"*The Asperkid's (Secret) Book of Social Rules* is a [r]
and teens with Asperger syndrome. By expo.
NTs and opening each chapter with a list of 'need-to-knows, ᴜ ...
sensitively and candidly explains the social rules that often confuse teens
with Asperger syndrome. The graphics, humor and short chapters make
the book lively and accessible, while O'Toole's own experiences as an
individual with Asperger syndrome help teens connect personally with her
insightful, practical advice."

—*Diane M. Kennedy and Rebecca S. Banks, authors of* Bright
Not Broken: Gifted Kids, ADHD, and Autism

"The joy of knowing that the mistakes of the past have a good chance of
melting away is the real, not-so-secret ingredient that makes this book shine."

—*Michael John Carley, Executive Director, GRASP, ASTEP,
and author of* Asperger's From the Inside Out

"Asperteens rejoice! Finally someone has produced a guide to the mysteries
of teenage social etiquette. Jennifer's brilliant writing style serves up huge,
life-changing advice in small, bite-sized chunks, making this an invaluable
reference point for navigating the difficult path between childhood and
adult life. If you're a teenager, buy a copy. If you're older, buy one too—it's
never too late to learn those 'secret rules' and apply them in your life."

—*Helen Wallace-Iles, founder and director, Autism All-Stars
UK, and mother of four children on the autism spectrum*

"Wow! This book is awesome. *The Asperkid's (Secret) Book of Social Rules* is a
triumph of words, wisdom and wit. It is a fun yet oh-so-important set of
keys that will help Asperkids of all ages unlock virtually every mystery the
NT world holds. I love it!"

—*Liane Holliday Willey, author of* Pretending to be
Normal *and* Safety Skills for Asperger Women

"Jennifer O'Toole has done it again. Reading this book was like dipping
into a bag of wonderful treasures. A very comprehensive guide to social
rules for Aspies and a brilliant reminder of just how much NTs take for
granted and how hard our Asperkids have to work each day. This book
serves as a 'universal translator' and will strengthen relationships between
Aspies and NTs everywhere… Our whole family is adopting the Asperkid
positivity vibe. Jennifer is like the favourite aunt and best friend we all wish
we had. If I could choose one book to give to my little boy as he grows
up, this would be it."

—*Rebecca Mitchell, psychotherapist (MBACP), author of the blog*
lovingmartians.wordpress.com, *and very proud mom to one
Asperboy superhero and his equally amazing NT supersister*

"Jennifer is the queen of understanding and helping others to understand the ins and out of Asperger syndrome. In this book Jennifer hits on all of the important issues tweens and teens face and provides ways for your Asperkids to thrive during this challenging time. Learn rules like 'to be interesting to other people, you first have to be interested in them,' 'one mistake does not a friendship break', 'being right isn't always the most important thing, even when it feels that way,' and so much more. As the mother of an eight-year-old with non-verbal learning disorder, ADD and SPD, this book is the first I grab to help both me and my amazing little gal. An incredible book by an incredible woman."

—*Lisa Davis, MPH, creator, host, and producer of It's Your Health Radio and It's Your Health TV*

"Not only is *The Asperkid's (Secret) Book of Social Rules* a book for Asperkid teens and tweens, it is also a book for their parents, caregivers and for anyone who grew up Aspie and wants to understand themselves and the world around them better. Being undiagnosed until in my 40s, this is the book I wish I had when I was a teenager. Thank you Jennifer, for not only making these social rules no longer 'secret' but for helping create a social survival guide that helps promote acceptance, enrichment, inspiration and empowerment for Asperkids everywhere!"

—*Karen Krejcha, Executive Director of Autism Empowerment, Aspie, GRASP 2012 DSM Award winner, and loving mom of two sons with autism and Asperger syndrome*

"There are so many reasons to love this book. It is kid-friendly, fun, packed with practical tips, and full of respect for those needing these tips the most. The thing I love best about it, however, is how appropriate the content is for every student, both those on the spectrum and those who are not. In fact, we can all learn something from Jennifer O'Toole's wonderful advice on relationships, organization, learning, communication and self-respect."

—*Paula Kluth, PhD, author of* You're Going to Love this Kid: Teaching Students with Autism in the Inclusive Classroom

The Asperkid's

- SECRET -

Book of Social Rules

by the same author

Asperkids
An Insider's Guide to Loving, Understanding and
Teaching Children with Asperger Syndrome
Jennifer Cook O'Toole
Foreword by Liane Holliday Willey
ISBN 978 1 84905 902 2
eISBN 978 0 85700 647 9

of related interest

Freaks, Geeks and Asperger Syndrome
A User Guide to Adolescence
Luke Jackson
Foreword by Tony Attwood
ISBN 978 1 84310 098 0
eISBN 978 1 84642 356 7

The Complete Guide to Asperger's Syndrome
Tony Attwood
ISBN 978 1 84310 495 7 (hardback)
ISBN 978 1 84310 669 2 (paperback)
eISBN 978 1 84642 559 2

Aspergirls
Empowering Females with Asperger Syndrome
Rudy Simone
Foreword by Liane Holliday Willey
ISBN 978 1 84905 826 1
eISBN 978 0 85700 289 1

Pretending to be Normal
Living with Asperger's Syndrome
Liane Holliday Willey
Foreword by Tony Attwood
ISBN 978 1 85302 749 9
eISBN 978 1 84642 210 2

The Asperkid's

- SECRET -

Book of Social Rules

The Handbook of Not-So-Obvious
Social Guidelines for Tweens and Teens
with Asperger Syndrome

Jennifer Cook O'Toole

Illustrated by Brian Bojanowski

Jessica Kingsley *Publishers*
London and Philadelphia

First published in 2013
by Jessica Kingsley Publishers
116 Pentonville Road
London N1 9JB, UK
and
400 Market Street, Suite 400
Philadelphia, PA 19106, USA

www.jkp.com

Copyright © Jennifer Cook O'Toole 2013
Illustrations copyright © Brian Bojanowski 2013

All rights reserved. No part of this publication may be reproduced in any material
form (including photocopying or storing it in any medium by electronic means and
whether or not transiently or incidentally to some other use of this publication)
without the written permission of the copyright owner except in accordance with the
provisions of the Copyright, Designs and Patents Act 1988 or under the terms of a
licence issued by the Copyright Licensing Agency Ltd, Saffron House, 6–10 Kirby
Street, London EC1N 8TS. Applications for the copyright owner's written permission
to reproduce any part of this publication should be addressed to the publisher.

Warning: The doing of an unauthorised act in relation to a copyright work may result
in both a civil claim for damages and criminal prosecution.

Library of Congress Cataloging in Publication Data
O'Toole, Jennifer Cook.
The Asperkid's (secret) book of social rules : the handbook of not-so-obvious social
guidelines for
tweens and teens with Asperger syndrome / Jennifer Cook O'Toole.
p. cm.
Includes bibliographical references.
ISBN 978-1-84905-915-2 (pbk. format : alk. paper) 1. Asperger's syndrome in
adolescence. 2.
Asperger's syndrome--Social aspects. 3. Asperger's syndrome--Patients--Life skills
guides. I. Title.
RJ506.A9O86 2012
618.92'858832--dc23
2012015213

British Library Cataloguing in Publication Data
A CIP catalogue record for this book is available from the British Library

ISBN 978 1 84905 915 2
eISBN 978 0 85700 685 1

Printed and bound in the United States

For Aspies of All Ages...
(and especially the ones in my house)

If you're not sure whether you believe in miracles,
perhaps you've forgotten that you are one.

You shall no longer take things at second or third hand,
nor look through the eyes of the dead,
nor feed on the spectres in books,
You shall not look through my eyes either,
nor take things from me,
You shall listen to all sides and filter them from your self.

Walt Whitman, "Song of Myself"

Contents

What You Need to Know about the Need-to-Knows: Making Sense of the Rules

Acknowledgments

There are times where you may find that you are part of something much bigger than yourself. For me, "right now" is such a time. And it is so very well with my soul. I am humbled by the voice I get to have in this world-wide "Aspie" conversation, and am honored to be given the chance to tie my life's experiences up in a bow and offer them, like a gift, to the next generation of Asperkids. So, thank you...

To the parents who've called me crying and afraid, and to the kids whose renewed self-esteem has made me burst with joy: thank you for sharing your journey and your trust. May I always do well by you.

To those who've taught me—through kindness or hurt, through love or abandonment—exactly who I am, thank you for showing me my own originality.

To the "Super Jessica" Kingsley (yes, I do think you should wear The Cape to board meetings) and her brilliant publishing team, thank you for believing in me—again. Know how sincerely I appreciate your vision and dedication and how proud I am to bear the JKP mark.

To Brian Bojanowksi—thank you for hours of sketching my crazy ideas and sometimes funny words into life. Thanks to Wendi and the boys for loaning you out, and thank you all for sharing the belief that this was never about us to begin with.

To my dear friends, Aileen, Lori, Amanda and Elizabeth, for continuing to encourage and support me always in all ways—no matter what life is throwing at you. I am inspired by each of you every single day.

To my mom. I know foreign languages were never your thing. So thank you, from the bottom of my heart, for trying so hard (for me and the kiddos) to learn to speak "Aspie." I love you and am so proud of you. Pink roses, Daddy. I miss you.

To my Asperkids, Maura (great cover idea!), Sean and Gavin (my little men): you rock. You are each such unique, precious bits of tomorrow. I fully expect you to change the world. Thank you for being mine.

Last, to my husband and best friend, John. I love you, Asperguy. Here's to a lifetime more of comfy routines, label-maker vs. Diet Coke can battles, and utter geek chic contentment. When it comes to being BFF, John, *we* wrote the book.

"Where was this Book When I, Like, Needed It?"

1990

Dear Journal,

What the heck? How is it possible to be so smart and so clueless at the exact same time? It seems like everyone else speaks a language that I don't. I watch them. I listen. I imitate. I act—a lot. Have you heard my newest nickname? The tennis team has taken to calling me "Happy Head." They actually mean it to be nice. I think I've become the seniors' pet. The cute little redhead with the smile plastered on her face—it's plastered, all right. And plastic. I'm completely petrified of feeling left out. Again. It's probably just a matter of time, though. We both know that I always manage to blow it somehow. Just give me long enough and I'll screw up any friendship. Seriously, I wish someone would just give me some rules on how to be "normal"...let me know when THAT book comes out. It seems to be the only one I haven't read.

Love,
Jenny

2012

There wasn't a Rule Book, then, like I wished. There was no peek into the secret rules that I knew had to be there, but couldn't ever figure out. There were rules, I was sure of it. Everyone else seemed to get them. But not me. Over and over, I'd mess up without even realizing it. Then try to cover it up. Then have to find new friends. For thirty-four years, that was the cycle, until I learned a new word: "Aspergers." And all of a sudden, I made sense. It all made sense. No, there wasn't a rule book then. But there is now. Part code-cracking, part doodle pad. Completely honest and all yours. Well, ours...

Welcome to the (Secret) Rule Book.

- Introduction -

Rules, Posers and Speaking a Foreign Language

We Aspies have a weird relationship with rules. In some ways, we love them. They kind of act like those organizing tubs you see in container stores. Sort this here, this does NOT go here, and move this out of the way. Rules aren't about telling us what NOT to do, as much as they tell us what we SHOULD do. They prevent chaos and confusion and stress. They create calm when the world feels messy and unpredictable. Rules, you might say, can be an Aspie's best friend.

On the other hand, we can take them a little bit overboard. "Rules" about healthy eating can become "food rituals" that restrict social activities; "rules" about homework can become perfectionism that causes great anxiety. Which is why the number one rule about rules is that they are almost never absolute. Confusing, but true. There are variables, exceptions and escape clauses, and you know what? No one gets this stuff right all the time. It's just that we Aspies like either/or a lot better than "sometimes" or "maybe." No big surprise that so many of us love games, hobbies and stories with predictable patterns and logical construction. Even our imaginations prefer facts and good versus evil basics: sci-fi, fantasy or historical fiction. What can I say? "Maybe" is just not our thing.

You've probably noticed by now that I'm saying "we," not "you." That's because I, too, am an Aspie. Although, if you're reading this, and you're an Asperkid, you have a major thing going for you already. You are SO lucky to *already* know what kind of mind you have. I didn't find out that I was an Aspie until I was an adult and learned that my own three kids (and husband) were Aspies, too. That means that I spent thirty-four years pretending to be just like everyone else. Which I wasn't. Growing up, I was "the brain." There was no word "Aspie" or "Asperkid," or anything else other than "dictionary head" and "know it all," and that kind of thing.

As I got older, I created myself on stage. Having started dancing at two, being on a stage in front of hundreds of people was, in many ways, a whole lot easier than being in a room with one person. If you have a script or choreographed dance steps, you just follow the plan. You can't really mess up—in fact, a very strange thing happens, or at least, it did for me. More and more, my real self popped through on stage, and the roles I played leaked into my daily life…until often I couldn't even tell when I was being real and when I was acting. I had enough scripts memorized and body language programmed into me that not only did I "act" well enough to blend in, I even became somewhat of a social butterfly.

Let me tell you, after all of that, I am one heck of an actress. I wore costumes in real life: cheerleader uniform, sorority letters, big hair (that was a good thing in the 1990s), and got so good at playing the "social game" that I earned the nickname "the flirt." At the time, that felt pretty cool—looking back, though, it was pretty sad. I didn't know I was an Asperkid. I just knew I'd spent enough years getting pranked, left out, made fun of and taunted. Enough nights crying at having to go back to school in the morning. Enough lunches hiding in the woods outside my high school rather than try to find a seat. So once I had the chance to play the role of "vamp" and "glamour girl," I took it for all it was worth—to extremes. Going from "nerd" to "hottie" felt like a promotion. It wasn't though, because either way, I was defining my self worth by someone else's label. I had no idea how to be authentic (a little nerdy, a little flirty) AND happy. So I'd play my "role" pretty well…but never convincingly enough to fluently "speak" neurotypical (NT). With no idea that I'd done something wrong, I'd bother, embarrass, annoy, hurt or disappoint someone. Through college, and in job after job afterwards, no matter what I achieved or where I managed to fit in, I always felt like a "poser," just waiting to be outed for the "fake" normal girl I was.

Less than two years ago, when I was identified as an Aspie, everything changed. Turned out, I wasn't defective, I was different. Being down on myself for making social blunders was as dumb as if I got mad at myself for having red hair or being a girl. We Aspies are hard-wired differently. Without trying, we can focus for hours on the tiniest details that other people seem to miss, and we understand wrong versus right down deep in our hearts. Being Aspie isn't bad or good, it just is. I will never be a brunette. I won't ever be male. And I am totally OK with both of those things. I'm also never going to be NT. It's not my normal. And if you are an Asperkid, it's not your normal either.

Part of understanding Aspie meant that I could forgive myself for messing up along the way. That was great. As my daughter said, "It means I'm not a dumb-bunny when it comes to people." No, she's not, I'm not, and you're not. But it also means that in order to get along in this world where most people's minds operate differently, we have to learn their rules. The problem is that nobody bothers to explain those rules to us—they just expect that we will "know" them, too. We learn manners, of course…or at least we should. Simply put, good manners make people more comfortable around us. They make other people feel good when they are around us—which means they WANT to be around us more. So? Sooo…if people want to be around us, it's easier to get help from teachers, find small group partners or gym teammates, get a date for the prom, even get hired for a job. Only as Asperkids, we don't think or learn or play like other kids. So we don't understand "manners"—or "secret rules"—the way that others do.

What Comes Naturally, and What Doesn't
Mind-Blindness

"Manners," generally speaking, are the traditions or customary ways a particular group has to guide the way people treat one another. Their purpose is to make social interaction smoother, less chaotic. Less about "me" and more about "we." And they change from society to society. So, in the Middle East, for example, to even show the bottom of your shoe to another human being is considered deeply offensive and rude. In Japan, not to take off your shoes upon entering a home would be the insult. In Bulgaria, nodding your head means "no" and shaking it from side to side says "yes," but the opposite is true most everywhere else. Argentinians expect you to arrive about thirty minutes after a set arrival time; many other cultures would find that disregard for time to be costly and arrogant. And in the United States, driving five miles over the speed limit is technically against the law—yet it's also expected, and sometimes even necessary if you don't want to tie up traffic.

Rules are relative, from one place to another. Expectations change over time (like women going to work), and from one situation to another (talking on a cell phone is fine, but not in the middle of a restaurant).

All this "fuzziness" confuses the heck out of us, right? Is someone being rude or just sarcastic? Or are they being sarcastic AND rude? Argh! Why can't this stuff just be simple? Why are these ridiculous "rules" secret to us, and not to the NTs?

Mostly, our trouble stems from two main challenges. The first is called "mind-blindness." That means that we have an awfully tough time figuring out someone else's point of view. Oh, we THINK we know what they are thinking…but usually, we don't, without actually asking.

Please get this. Mind-blindness doesn't mean Aspies are uncaring. Once we find out someone has been hurt, or is afraid or alone, we can be the most sympathetic people around. That's compassion: feeling sorrow or pity for someone else's misfortune. Heck, I couldn't even read *Charlotte's Web* (White 1952) as a kid, and I still have to actually get up and run to turn off the television if a commercial for hunger relief or animal safety comes on. My heart can't take the ache I feel. Strangely, my own son, an Asperkid, does the same thing when he knows the plot of a cartoon will involve a character's feelings being hurt. He runs. My dad, definitely an Asperguy, used to walk out of a room if anyone cried. He wasn't cold. I think it was the opposite. The feelings were just too big.

As for me, my first job out of college was as a social worker helping kids in violent homes and then as a teacher for students who felt lost, dumb or left out. The underdog was always my favorite, and probably always will be. So never ever let anyone tell you that Aspies don't feel great love for others. They couldn't be more wrong. We may look like we aren't feeling a thing, but you and I know that couldn't be further from the truth.

On the other hand, sympathy and empathy are very different things. Sympathy we've got in spades. Empathy, which is the ability to sense, be aware of and share another's feelings is, let's admit it, not our collective strong point. Compassionate though we may be, we Aspies usually have to really ponder or even be directly told what someone else's perspective might be. It's not something we're naturally aware of. That doesn't make us bad or mean or uncaring. It means that we have to think about what NTs just "get."

On the flip side, we often "get" things that NTs have to stress over, study and try desperately to memorize. Neither brain is better. They're just different ways a mind can work. And just like an NT might have to buckle down to even have a chance at remembering a timeline or equation or factoid you know by rote, we have to "do our homework" to learn the social rules that run our mostly neurotypical world.

Impulsivity—AKA "Oops"

I'm speaking from personal experience when I say that we Aspies can be, shall we say, a tad bit impulsive? Ever open your mouth, say exactly what you meant not to say, and then spend the rest of the day beating yourself up for it? I have. Frequently.

So even when we *do* figure out another person's perspective and how we may be affecting her, we often react before we give ourselves time to think. And usually, speaking or behaving impulsively doesn't come out the way we want. Those would be our "Oops, I over-shared again" or "I cannot believe I just said that" socially awkward moments.

When my daughter was little, I taught her a trick with mazes. Start at the end, then work your way backwards. If you know where you're going, you can plan your route much more effectively. It's true for most anything in life. If you want to visit China, a guide to traveling through Costa Rica isn't going to be much help.

If you want to make a fabulous dinner, you're going to have a much better chance of getting the necessary ingredients from the grocery store if you know that your end product should be curried chicken and not spaghetti and meatballs.

That's just real. For us, "playing well with others" isn't impossible at all, it just takes a whole lot more thinking, strategizing and planning than it does for NTs. But if we're not careful, our impulsivity can sabotage our best social efforts before we've really begun.

Learning to Speak "Social-Ease"

All that thinking and planning and confusion may lead you to think, why bother? This is all just too much work. Forget it. I get that. I have been there. Actually, I still am there sometimes. It's probably one of my favorite things about having (accidentally?) married an Aspie and having Asperkids. We understand one another without having to do a lot of explaining or figuring. But that sure wasn't true of my life growing up. And it still isn't true the minute I walk out my door.

So, the truth is that you don't HAVE to learn the rules if you don't want to. It's really your choice. But…as with any choice, there are consequences. If you want a career, a date, an invitation, a friend or even to get along with the NTs in your family…you have to learn their language. "Social-ease." You may never be fluent, and you may always have an "Aspie accent," but at least you'll know what to (try) to say.

Just imagine moving to some other country and being expected to speak their language, know the customs and follow every one of their super-complicated laws—without anyone ever explaining them to you. And if you mess up, you could (and probably would) get fired, be laughed at, left out, bullied, or even arrested. Would that be fair? Of course not.

But that's what it's like for us, trying to follow a set of **hidden social rules** without the rule book. To us, they're not rules, they're secrets. It's no wonder we feel left out so often. You won't just "know" things that are not part of the way you, as Asperkids, operate…any more than I will suddenly know what it's like to wake up blonde. Someone's got some explaining to do.

Social psychologists try. They are scientists who study the way people interact and develop connections, using fancy terms like "social norm" (think "normal") to describe hidden rules. The scientists say that people observe each other, and then think about each other. Those thoughts lead to feelings. And then people behave based on their feelings. It's a cycle: NTs *observe, think, feel* and *act*.

"Secret" rules are just part of that big cause and effect deal. How "well" you follow the rules (the cause) determines how most NTs will treat you (the effect). **Do what others expect, and the reward is that you are accepted by the group. Do it any other way, and people (kids and adults) feel threatened, uncomfortable, even embarrassed or scared.** So they freak. And all sorts of lousy consequences—bullying, teasing, practical jokes, etc.—act like a punishment. "Get in line or else" is the basic message. And it doesn't change as you grow up.

Hold the Pillow

OK, we have arrived at our first "hold the pillow" moment. I know you have no idea what that means. Just stick with me. A psychiatrist friend of mine, Dr. Irm Bellavia, showed me a great visual. She'd ask an Asperkid to imagine that the little throw pillows on her office couch were important—but tough—things that he had to hear. Not mean. Not put-downs. Just real stuff. Then, she'd toss the pillows at him, one at a time. At first, they'd bounce off—he wouldn't be expecting them. Maybe he'd then even throw them back. Eventually, she'd say "Catch it. Hold on." And she'd just wait. And he'd hold the pillow. That's what all of us have to be able to do—to hold on and hear that we might be wrong, or if not wrong, maybe not exactly helping ourselves out.

We don't have the "Social-ease" dictionary programmed into our brains; NTs do. They are constantly "taking the social temperature." Without even realizing it, NTs monitor each other's body language and tone of voice—able to correctly detect what others think of them. If NTs sense they are causing uncomfortable or confused thoughts or feelings, they can change their own behavior in time to keep everyone comfortable and happy.

For us Aspies, that's not a natural skill. We either don't notice or don't understand the thoughts we make others think about us. Growing up, I was bullied, teased, left out…you name it. Not my fault. BUT. (I am holding the pillow here!) Looking back, I can see that I did not help myself. In fact, without even realizing it, I absolutely can see that I did a lot of things to come off as a know-it-all, bossy, snobby, whatever. I didn't understand how I made other people think about me.

When we act in ways that are unexpected, other people feel uncomfortable about us (that can look like frustration, uncertainty, embarrassment, confusion). And when they feel uncomfortable, they are going to behave in ways that will try to get the person who created that feeling to either go away or change.

They may even become aggressive, if only to make themselves feel more in control again. That's where the bullying comes in. If you feel "on the edge" or left out or hurt, it isn't your fault. Period. You didn't ask for it, and you don't have to just take it. But if there are things you are doing, social "rules" you are breaking without meaning to—don't you want to know? There may be some things you can do to keep everyone more comfortable in the first place. You're not to change who you are. Ever. For anyone. You're just going to learn some of the "NT customs" to make your life in NT world a bit easier.

The (Secret) Book

Right after I was diagnosed, I started writing a rule book. It began as a tool for myself that I assembled by watching "people patterns." I noticed that, taken up close, the NT world wasn't quite as random as I'd thought. In fact, there seemed to be trends… actual rules that could be inferred by careful study.

If there wasn't a rule book for the "obvious" things, I'd have to write one. And for good measure, I'd try to figure out the beliefs behind the rules—if only to understand the logic and make the idea stick. We Aspies are big on logic. Give us the reason and we will follow the rule, even if it doesn't come naturally. But if we see no point, well, that's going to be a lot tougher.

So, I found myself a blank notebook and wrote down some "apparent" rules. I was my own test case. And lo and behold, the "rules" worked. No, the responses weren't huge celebrations or applause. I knew they worked when NTs didn't realize I was doing anything at all. When I, like a cloaked, undercover Aspie spy, infiltrated the everyday NT world and flew (mostly) under the social radar. Instead of ruffled feathers or hurt feelings, there was calm and respect. The (Secret) Rule Book was born.

Almost immediately after I started writing, my kids wanted their own version of the rules. In particular, my daughter pointed out, when I explained the rule to her I always illustrated it with a story. So those had better be included. I don't think it hurt, by the way, that usually the story involved me (aka Mom) in a less-than-fabulous-often-humiliating moment. I get it. No one likes to feel preached at. Aesop used animals to take the sting out of his lessons. I am about to use a whole boatload of embarrassing stories.

Now, they belong to you, too. Pieced together from careful observations (and a whole lot of mess-ups), these are some of the most important "NT rules" that Asperkids need to know.

What's Ahead

- **138 Need-to-Know Rules in Bullet Points** for you to peruse and go back to for reminders whenever you want.

- **31 mini-chapters about those Need-to-Knows**; NT rules don't make sense to us without explanation, so this is where I do the NT-to-Aspie translating for you.

- **Stickies** are super-short, sticky-note-sized pointers that didn't need more explaining, but they sure needed to be said.

- **Practice Sessions** are six comic strips where you can see our detective work in action.

- **Stick a Fork in It** and **Resources You Will Actually WANT to Use** are how I am going to send you out into the world, feeling proud, ready and AWESOME.

Every single "hidden" or "secret" rule is something I wish someone had told me when I was younger—something I teach my own Asperkids, and am so excited to share with you, too. I'm not promising a life of perfect sailing, sunshine, puppies and lollipops. You may think you're got a "rule" down pat, then one or two things change and you feel like you're back to square one. It's OK. That's true even for NTs, I promise.

Some rules may seem easy to you. Others won't. Use this book in pieces, take your time, and forgive yourself if you mess up. We all mess up. If you want perfect, you won't find it in *this* book. What you will find is a lot of honesty from me to you. And a whole lot of embarrassing stories—my own. Listen, I'm older than you, but I'm an Aspie, too. I'm not about to preach to you like I have absolutely everything perfectly together. I figure, if you're going to put yourself out there and bravely listen to what I have to say, then you at least deserve to laugh at some of my own cringe-worthy moments.

The honest truth is that you also may not agree with a particular "rule" or social expectation. I remember once writing an entire history essay about why I felt the essay question itself was wrong. That's where the idea of "it is what it is" comes in. Sometimes a rule just is. And there is your choice. You can say, "Whatever," and walk away…as long as you are willing to accept the consequences. Otherwise, it is what it is. Like it or not, the rule's the rule.

Aspie Forever

Most importantly, do not try to be something or someone you are not. Ever. Remember what I said about my always feeling like a "poser," a fraud? That's a horrible way to live. These rules aren't going to turn you "poof!" into an NT. Which is a good thing. Being an Asperkid isn't something to hide—actually, it's something to laugh about and even be proud of. It puts you in the company of minds like Thomas Edison, Bill Gates, Marie Curie.

Information, more often than not, brings about understanding. My kids and I have found being honest about who we are and how we operate is the way to go. You may want to ask your psychologist to speak to your class about Aspergers. About how it's just a different way brains can work—no better or worse, just different. You know: how we're great at staying focused on something that's important to us, but otherwise may be a bit scattered or need our space. My daughter's therapist came to speak in her class, and the students (and teachers) really appreciated it. The kids even called her "brave," and shared stories about Aspies in their own families.

If kids react well to learning about Aspergers, they're the kind you want around you. If they are anything less than kind, then you're better off spending your time elsewhere anyway. You deserve that kind of respect, too. "Pretending to be normal" is not only exhausting, it's sad. So, be who you are without apologies, and use the rules to help you get along the best you can with the NTs around you.

Whatever you decide about "telling" or not, it's your call. Just remember that these rules are not—I repeat NOT—about trying to pretend to be anyone other than you. They are about helping you—well—us—feel more confident in the friendships we make and the people we are. If you are Irish and move to the United States or vice versa, you are going to speak the same language, but always with a different accent. That's like NTs who try to "get" Aspie. Or Aspies who work the hidden NT social rules. We never lose our identity. We just learn to communicate better. You don't have to like everyone, and no matter what you do, everyone will not like you. We do, however, all need to learn to "play nicely" when life sticks us together. And it will continue to stick us together.

After you've read this book, go back and read it again. Experience will keep handing you the same lesson over and over until you learn what you need to. Have you seen playgrounds where the ground is covered in cushiony, recycled rubber stuff? The world isn't like that. It's a lot more like old-fashioned blacktop. You will, at one time or another, trip and fall and skin your knee. You will make mistakes. What will you do? Sit there? Cry? Scream? What I want for you to do, instead, is to stand up, brush off the gravel, and keep moving. Fall down seven times, get back up seven times. And think of me as your helping hand— something to grab hold of to pull yourself up.

My original rule book has a proverb printed on the cover. It reads, "Just when the caterpillar thought everything was all over, it spread its wings and became a butterfly." There have been many times I wished I could crawl in a hole and hide. There are still some memories that make me flinch now, years later. Yet never did I, in fact, actually die of embarrassment. You are no different. Like that caterpillar, without a copy of the rules, we have no idea what to expect. But give us the playbook everyone else has, and we've got a chance to fly.

If, in the end, you can't remember any of the other rules that follow, please learn this one—write it out on a piece of paper, tape it to your bathroom mirror, whatever you need to do—just memorize it. From one (albeit grown-up) Asperkid to another:

You are exactly who and how you were meant to be.

You may make mistakes, but YOU are not a mistake.

And the world is better already, just because you've arrived.

Need-to-Knows

The Unspoken Rules—In Bullet Points

- Persistence means dedication even when you royally and publicly mess up.
- Skill develops over time, not overnight.
- Everything is hard before it becomes easy.
- Failure hurts. But it's the best way to learn.
- When you feel trapped in your mistakes is exactly when you have to start getting creative.
- Success is about what you do when—not if—you fail.
- The biggest mistake you can make is being too afraid to make one.
- Whenever you *think* you should say thank you, you probably should.
- "Thank you" is a reward that encourages a particular behavior to continue.
- Failing to recognize others' words or actions makes us seem unappreciative.
- "Notice, Tell, Thank" is the simple step-by-step process to letting people know they matter.
- "Thank-Yous" come in different levels, and NTs will expect you to know which kind is right for each situation.
- Sometimes, saying "thank you" is enough. Other times, more is expected.

- "Notice, Tell, Thank" works in written thank-yous as well.
- Written thank-yous can be sent as handwritten notes, e-cards and digital photo cards, or emails, depending on the type of note and who is receiving it.
- Thank-you gifts are the way to go when someone does something extra special for you.
- Never let your thank-you gift outshine the original gift.
- "I'm sorry" don't have to be the hardest words to say. But they are some of the most important.
- Apologies don't make one person a winner and the other a loser.
- A good apology says what went wrong, which feelings got hurt, and what should've happened instead.
- One mistake does not a friendship break.
- Forgiving isn't the same as forgetting.
- Being right isn't always the most important thing, even when it feels that way.
- How you correct an error (humbly, in private) is as important as whether you correct it.
- Peers don't like to be corrected by one another.
- Unless there's danger, never correct an adult or authority figure.
- Knowing when, how or if you should point out someone's mistake isn't easy, but it is doable.
- Wanting to be excellent is good. Wanting to improve is great. Wanting to be perfect is arrogant.
- Perfectionism makes any amount of success worthless compared to a single failure.
- Our perfectionism comes across to other people as annoying, smug superiority.

- Other people want to be able to relate to you. No one can relate to "perfect."
- It can be hard to tell the difference between playful teasing, mean teasing and accidental hurts.
- Aspies tend to take ourselves super-seriously. That's not the same as being "too sensitive."
- Ask yourself: Do I trust the person who is teasing me? Would they really want to hurt me? Perhaps we're mis-communicating.
- Everyone wants to feel heard and to know that they matter.
- Show what you know bit-by-bit so that everyone gets a chance to be heard.
- To be interesting to other people, you first have to be interested in them.
- You have to use your whole body to SHOW someone you are truly listening (remember: they can't tell you are paying attention unless you SHOW it).
- Reflective listening techniques help you stay focused and create strong connections with other people.
- Compliments given to others aren't insults to you.
- Being able to give sincere compliments is the surest way to receive them.
- Specific compliments are the strongest.
- Graciously accept compliments with a simple smile and "thank you."
- Leaders listen to others' ideas and respect them. Their minds are "flexible," like wet spaghetti.
- Being a rigid thinker ("my way is the only right way") is like being uncooked spaghetti. You break (or break down) when you're asked to change.
- Change is the only thing that is certain.

- If we can only handle the world as we expect it to be, we are going to snap, just like uncooked spaghetti.
- "Small group work" is a lifelong experience—it doesn't end after school does.
- How you say something is as important as what you say.
- Different doesn't mean wrong. There is usually more than one way to solve a problem well.
- Everyone feels that he or she is the most important, most interesting person in the world.
- Don't always say what *you* want to say or what *you* are feeling. Ask yourself what *the other person* might be feeling. And respond to *that*.
- No one enjoys criticism, but nothing improves without it.
- Black-and-white thinking (being uncooked spaghetti) can make it hard to really listen to a critique.
- "Old wounds" from bullying may make criticism feel like an actual attack, even if no one is actually out to hurt us.
- We have to be able to "hold the pillow" to learn and grow as people.
- Criticism can bring you down. It can also build you up.
- Diffuse criticism from people you don't trust. Seek it out from people you do.
- The more defensively you react to criticism, the more likely it is true.
- Take a breath, "hold the pillow," listen and learn.
- Avoid giving criticism if you can.
- If it is kind, true and necessary, you still have to package it well.
- Stay positive and specific, and always offer a solution.
- Critique ideas and actions rather than people.
- Sandwich everything between sincere compliments.

- NTs don't always mean what they say, especially when asking for "honest" opinions.

- NTs usually believe that lying is wrong UNLESS it is done to spare others' feelings or make a good impression.

- NTs tell "white" lies frequently—which is tough on Aspies, who take most everything at face value.

- Be sure to only trust those who have earned your confidence. You'll be taken advantage of otherwise.

- Tact is knowing how, when, or whether to say what we are thinking.

- Being honest isn't the same as speaking every thought in your head.

- Before speaking, ask yourself: Is it true? Is it good or kind? Is it useful or necessary?

- Aspies take things literally—but NTs don't speak literally. What they say and what they mean are not always the same thing.

- It's OK to get confused. We're not hard-wired to understand language the way NTs use it.

- Build yourself a team of trustworthy, patient NT "advisors." You can check in with them if you feel confused about a social situation.

- Aspies' black-and-white extreme-kind-of-thinking often leads us to believe problems are MUCH bigger than they actually are.

- We can go from Worry Level 1 to Worry Level 100 in a split second. This helps NOBODY, most especially ourselves.

- Stop panicking. Breathe. Look at the steps in your "Chain of Catastrophe"—and ask "Why might this *not* happen?"

- Empower yourself by imagining steps you can take to make things better.

- All conflicts have history. The time to act is before meltdowns occur.

- NTs don't understand that we melt down because we are feeling overwhelmed.

- We must clearly communicate and problem solve when we are calm. No one listens when we yell.

- Our bodies give us signals before a meltdown. Pay attention and choose to respond in a proactive way.

- Anticipate sensory overload and use your coping skills to relax and re-direct your energy.

- Tomorrow *is* another day.

- "Hygiene" comes from the name "Hygeia," the ancient Greek goddess of good health (best friend of the goddess of love and beauty).

- To be healthy, you have to be clean.

- NT world truth: people are going to judge you by how you present yourself.

- Being messy sends NTs the message that you are disorganized and irresponsible.

- Being clean makes you more pleasant to be around and more attractive to others.

- Personal grooming should happen and be discussed in private.

- Aspies' mind-blindness keeps us from seeing boundaries between our ideas, feelings, bodies and possessions and other people's.

- Other people's feelings are as real to them as yours are to you.

- When we cross those invisible lines, we make NTs feel threatened, violated or offended.

- To protect themselves from further discomfort, they push "outsiders" away.

- Learning where NTs' boundaries are will help keep them comfortable around us and treating us well.
- The NT world has lots of "invisible" boundaries around friendships.
- You need to know exactly what a friend *is*, not just what a friend *isn't*.
- Carefully and purposefully choose the people in your life.
- Friendships aren't perfect because people aren't perfect. Even true friends make mistakes sometimes.
- A worthwhile friendship is one which makes you feel good about being you.
- NTs see friendship in levels. Knowing them helps us to know who to trust and how much to trust them.
- It's better to be without a friend than to be mistreated by someone who says they are a friend.
- Keep friendships and conversations balanced; coming on too strong makes NTs uncomfortable.
- Friendships require more attention as they become more important.
- Honestly knowing your strengths and needs is like having a superpower.
- Anger is a band-aid emotion. It's a real thing—but the wound you have to heal is underneath the anger.
- We teach others how they may treat us. We must respect ourselves before they will respect us.
- Self-advocacy means clearly expressing your rights in a calm way.
- Judging your own value by how many people "like" you is a recipe for failure.
- You must be the first to respect yourself.
- Having dignity means that you will NOT cooperate with anything or anyone that humiliates you.

- If you believe you are worthy and strong, you will live up to that truth. If you believe you are unworthy of love or happiness, you will live up to that truth, too.

- NTs say confidence and dignity are the most attractive qualities someone can have.

- Before you send a text or email to anyone, ask yourself: Is it true? Is it kind or good? Is it useful or necessary?

- People on the other side of the computer are real, with real feelings, real opinions and real reactions. However, the feelings, opinions and reactions they show online may not be real.

- What you write, text or post will ALWAYS be copy-and-pasteable, quotable, sharable and traceable.

- All "friends" are not all equal. Levels of friendship still exist in cyberspace.

- Avoid texting important conversations about the beginning or end of relationships, medical diagnoses or other major life events.

- Keep the amount of contacts when messaging, emailing, texting and posting balanced; reciprocity rules online, too.

- To the right girl or guy, your quirky self is the most attractive person in the world.

- No guy or girl is worth crying over. And the one who is won't make you cry.

- Nothing is more attractive than confidence, courtesy and self-respect.

- "Beautiful" and "hot" are NOT the same thing.

- Being a "lady" means having self-respect and confidence.

- Being a "gentleman" means having common sense and good manners.

- Aspies see beauty in pieces and parts; NTs prefer to focus on the total picture.

- The NT world expects us to get the "big idea" or "gestalt."
- Active Listening Skills ("Mirror! Mirror!") and Signal Words help you hear someone's main idea.
- "Palm Reading" can help you find the main idea in anything written.
- You must be able to accurately take information in to be able to support your own ideas and opinions.
- Aspies are prime targets for bullies because we are different and often defenseless.
- Tattling is meant to get someone in trouble. Telling is meant to get someone help (including yourself).
- You are only in charge of what YOU do. Unless someone could get hurt or is being bullied, don't be the "police officer."
- Bullying is about taking your POWER away. Telling is about taking it back.
- Bullying among girls is really complicated. Aspergirls and their families should read *Queen Bees and Wannabes* to understand the roles girls play in NT cliques.
- Laughing at your *mistake* is NOT the same as laughing at *you*.
- The NT world considers laughing at your own blunders to be one of the "highest" kinds of humor.
- An action may be funny. A person is not. The joke is what you did, it isn't who you are.
- Do not make fun of your own pain just so it's not so bad when others hurt you. It doesn't work and it costs you self-respect.
- NTs perceive those who can laugh at themselves as secure, confident, strong and likable.
- A person who isn't afraid to tease him or herself makes a connection with everyone listening.
- No one can laugh at you if you're already laughing.

What You Need to Know about the Need-to-Knows

Making Sense of the Rules

1

How Not to Make a Light Bulb

Why Everything is Hard Before It is Easy

From The Desk Of:
Thomas Edison

Inventor's Notebook:

Method #894 on how
NOT to make a
light bulb.

Need-to-Knows

- Persistence means dedication even when you royally and publicly mess up.
- Skill develops over time, not overnight.

- Everything is hard before it becomes easy.

- Failure hurts. But it's the best way to learn.

- When you feel trapped in your mistakes is exactly when you have to start getting creative.

- Success is about what you do when—not if—you fail.

- The biggest mistake you can make is being too afraid to make one.

Asperkid Logic

Have you ever watched a toddler who is learning how to walk? It's a very clumsy thing. No matter how strong or how sturdy he is, no matter how smart or how coordinated she seems, every single little kid falls. A lot. There are a lot of skinned knees and split lips. And suddenly, everything in the house is geared toward preventing a trip to the emergency room. Diapers serve double duty as tush padding. Baby gates suddenly appear everywhere. Table corners are covered with foam bumpers. Catalogs offer baby crash helmets, and even mini elbow or knee pads. There are even "professionally certified babyproofers" (I am being completely serious, people) who, for several thousands of dollars at a time, promise to help safeguard toddlers as they, well, toddle around their homes.

OK. Got it. Learning to walk is a super-huge life moment, an enormous business, and very ungraceful. So?

Well here's my question to you: do you remember learning to walk? Of course not. Yet you obviously did it at some point. And it was a big deal to your little baby self (this was serious exercise and not a little bit frustrating). You wanted to check out some shiny thing or reach that cracker. You didn't want to wait for somebody to get your favorite stuffed animal or hand you a sippy cup. You wanted it, and you wanted it NOW. You wanted to be part of the fun. Maybe follow your dog or your brother. There may have been times when you screamed your head off in frustration. Or maybe you sat and thought about it, trying to plan your next daring escape from the crib. Whatever you did, the fact is that for a good long time, no matter how badly you wanted to walk, you just couldn't.

This whole walking thing was also a big deal to everyone watching close by—those people who cared about you, helped you up if you stumbled, and cheered when you tried again. They may have even made home movies as you pulled yourself up, cruised along the furniture, carefully tried to balance…and then fell flat on your face. Repeatedly. Eventually, though, you got strong enough and had enough experience in what NOT to do to manage to keep your balance for a step, or even two. And within a matter of days if not weeks, your wobbly toddle became a "Frankenstein-ish" waddle and then a ridiculously fast (though not at all coordinated) run that probably terrified your parents all over again.

If someone were to watch that last bit, it might have even seemed that Baby You went from floor-bound crawler to nutty little marathon kid practically overnight. But you didn't. Don't forget the face-plants and split lips, the safety gates and bruised tush. No, this wasn't an overnight success. It was hard-won and worked at—by a small child, yes, but an achievement made no less worthy or admirable because of your age.

That's why you need look no further than your first triumph to remember this rule: **everything is hard before it becomes easy**. That's true for walking, talking, riding a bike, driving a car, doing multiplication, figuring out irregular verbs, quantum mechanics, going on a date, job interviews, and everything else that comes along. Life, in general, takes persistence. Which doesn't just mean long periods of dedication. **Persistence means dedication even when you royally and publicly mess up.** It means falling on your face and getting hurt. Feeling completely mortified when someone (or everyone) sees you topple over. Walking into a party with your skirt tucked into your underwear (OK, that might have happened to me), then getting over it, NOT running away, and sticking around to try again.

As one of my favorite TV characters of all times (and a total Aspie), Dr. Gregory House, said, **"If you are not willing to look stupid, nothing great is ever going to happen to you."**

Television talent shows make a huge industry out of taking folks and turning them into superstars. Of course, they don't show the backstory—hours of music lessons or practicing scales or getting laughed off stage. They don't show that because it's long and not too exciting to watch. But those bumpy days happened. **Because *everything* is hard before it becomes easy. Skill develops over time, not overnight.**

Being patient can be really hard—I know—especially when it comes to what we, Aspies, expect of ourselves. Ever try a new kind of math equation and end up completely furious with yourself, or lose it when you didn't "get" a new lesson immediately? What about trying to learn to jump rope and being the only one in the class who couldn't get the hang of it? (My hand's up, here.) Usually, this is when Asperkids want to quit…or scream…or just freak out at anyone who gets in their way.

Exactly why, though, should we know how to do something expertly right away? How come we think that—unlike everyone else—we don't need to put in time and effort before we are able to do (or maybe even fabulously achieve) something? The answer, of course, is that we can't do everything well the first time we try. And we shouldn't expect ourselves to. EVERYTHING is hard before it is easy…for a reason. **If you can stick around through feeling embarrassed or disappointed or frustrated, there is something to be gained in the time it takes to learn.** Something you can't gain any other way. Character and creativity. Resilience. Winston Churchill, that great, stubborn force, famously said, **"Success is not final, failure is not fatal; it is the courage to continue that counts"** (Vilord 2002, p.36).

As a baby, your legs got stronger by having to get back up over and over again. Your arms got more flexible from having to pull back up. Your reflexes got faster at detecting off-kilter balance only from learning what it felt like to fall. So, yes, this rule is partially about being nicer to yourself, and being more forgiving of mistakes. And it is partially about tossing the idea that anyone else thinks you ought to do everything right the first time. They don't (really) and you shouldn't (really).

Somewhere, we get this crazy idea in our heads that smart people or cool people or people who are just generally worth having around don't fail. Wrong. They do. Happy people, content people…they just won't allow a blunder to be their final statement. **The biggest mistake you can make is being too afraid to make one.**

"No" or "you're wrong" or complete and total public humiliation—as awful as they feel at the time (and I am so agreeing that they DO feel awful)—can give you the chance to do and imagine and be things you never imagined. Give yourself a little time to see what can happen. **When you feel trapped in your mistakes is exactly when you have to start getting creative. It's when you really get to see the genius you have inside.**

The fact is that everyone—EVERYONE—messes up. Fails, even. That's not what determines who succeeds in life and who doesn't. In fact, many people will let early successes give them a false sense of confidence, that everything will come easily to them. Like I did at dance.

I started dance at age two, and right from the beginning, I was really good at it. It felt wonderful and without much effort, I could do whatever my teachers asked, and more. So pretty quickly, I just took for granted that dance would always be a no-brainer for me. Then, somewhere around age thirteen, I had the chance to audition for my first off-Broadway company. Everyone in the room was older than me, they filled out their leotards a lot differently, and they just seemed to walk around like they owned the place. I was totally psyched out.

So it's probably no big surprise that when the choreographer broke us into trios, demonstrated the combination we were to instantly absorb and then turned us loose to show her what we could do, I choked. I can't even remember if I managed a leap or a turn. All I know is that I ran out of the room crying. I wasn't upset about not making the company or even about looking ridiculous in front of everyone else (OK, maybe a little bit about that—although they'd all probably done the same thing at some point).

Nope. I was humiliated and angry and furious with myself because I hadn't gotten it right immediately, as I always had before, and as other people had that day.

Here's what I didn't realize, though. Yes, I had the ability to dance as well as any of those older kids. My teacher wouldn't have invited me to audition otherwise. But what they had on their side was time and experience. The experience of having attended more rehearsals, auditions and call-backs. Of trying out and getting cut, of feeling the surge of determination and then showing up to try again. Their failures made them better dancers. Maybe not technically. But in confidence, maturity and grace, absolutely.

So, I changed my game plan. The next audition I had, I prepared like crazy beforehand—and nailed the lead...a role which changed my life for the better in a million ways...a role for which I'd never have auditioned if I'd gotten the first part.

No, the difference between who reaches their dreams and who doesn't isn't about how well you begin. **Success is about what you do when—not if—you fail.** The ones who bounce back, who keep trying...they will triumph. One of the most famous players in the history of American baseball (my favorite sport) was the New York Yankees' Babe Ruth. By the time he retired in 1935, he had hit more home runs of any other player, a record that stood until 1961. He also had struck out the most times. If Ruth had let all of his "failures" distract him, though, he never would have kept swinging for the fences—and never would have become a legend in his own time.

Want some more proof that messing up doesn't mean you're a mess up? Done. Here are a few famous examples of "suspected-Aspies" who didn't get it right at first, but sure got it right in the end:

- **Henry Ford**—Yup, he eventually invented American-made cars (among other things), but the founder of the Ford Motor Company lost all of his money FIVE times before succeeding.

- **Thomas Edison**—He was told by his teacher that he was too stupid to learn anything. Before he invented a working light bulb, he failed about 1000 times. But Edison said they weren't failures. Newspapers of the times report he insisted, "We now know 1000 ways not to build a light bulb" (Vilord 2002, p.78). Maybe not so dumb after all.

- **Emily Dickinson**—One of the most famous American poets of all time, she only managed to have a few dozen poems published during her lifetime. Still, she didn't stop writing as long as she lived…thanks to her tireless work, more than 1800 of her completed pieces are in print today.

- **Bill Gates**—Did you know he dropped out of Harvard and bombed the first time he started a computer company? Traf-O-Data isn't quite a household name, is it? He seems to have done pretty well with the Microsoft thing, though.

- **Albert Einstein**—He didn't speak until age four, or read until age seven (he was dyslexic), and was eventually expelled from school. I'm guessing that the Nobel Prize for changing the entire understanding of modern physics and the fabric of the universe made up for it, though.

Such is the value of the learning curve. **If everything came easily right away, we'd take for granted our successes, victories, skills and talents.** Not to mention that we'd have little respect for people (you know, Einstein and friends) who have invested the time and effort that we haven't.

No one succeeds all of the time. No one. What makes some people special…timeless…courageous is their willingness to keep trying and never, ever give up.

So the next time you try to pronounce a foreign word in front of your class and flub it, breathe easy. Your voice cracks in chorus tryouts? It's no biggie. You try for a double-jumping-front-kick at karate and manage to land right on your back? You'll live. There aren't safety gates near your stairs anymore, are there? Nope. Eventually, you learned to walk. And eventually, you *will* say that word, hit that note, nail that move. And you'll be a much stronger person for having messed up in the process.

2

The Potty-Training Rule

Knowing When a Thank-You is Expected

Need-to-Knows

- Whenever you *think* you should say thank you, you probably should.

- "Thank you" is a reward that encourages a particular behavior to continue.

- Failing to recognize others' words or actions makes us seem unappreciative.

- "Notice, Tell, Thank" is the simple step-by-step process to letting people know they matter.

Asperkid Logic

Ever since you were little, you've known that saying please and thank you is simply good manners. And that's true. But you're older now, which means "thank you" is about much more than just being polite. **Being able to say "thank you" at the right time and in the right way is an important unspoken rule with a lot riding on it.**

Whoopee. I can practically see you rolling your eyes. Next rule, please—let's skip ahead. Just give me a second, though. Everyone—Aspies included—deserves to be appreciated and to feel important. And that's what a good "thank you" does.

Let's think of a "thank-you" as a reward. That's actually the way social scientists describe it. Really. Basically, the idea is that by (1) showing your appreciation and respect, you (2) create positive feelings in the other person, and (3) reinforce the specific behavior (keep being nice to me!). In other words, saying thank you will make people want to be friendly again to you in the future.

Now Aspies have manners that are as good as anyone's. It's not so much the act of giving thanks that we Aspies miss. We miss the step before that. Often, we don't notice what we're even supposed to be saying thank you for.

Experts say that one of the most forgotten social skills is simple appreciation. And paying attention to someone else's words or actions can be really tough for Asperkids (and adults). Remembering to look for and then trying to figure out the thoughts and effort *behind* the words and actions is even tougher.

Let's say you have a new video game, and you are in the middle of the highest scoring round you've ever played. In that case, the call to the dinner table doesn't feel like an invitation to share time and food. It feels like an interference. You don't want to have to stop. Which means you're probably not going to gracefully notice that there is a hot dinner in front of you which was not, in fact, synthesized by a "food replicator." Someone earned the money to buy the food, and took the time to plan, shop for, and prepare the meal. That's awfully hard to remember, though, when all you can think of is the video game.

Or if you are caught up in your newest Lego masterpiece, you may not care that your dad rearranged his schedule to be able to drive you to school. When it's time to go, you're just frustrated that you have to stop.

While no one may ever call your feelings wrong, it's quite possible that they're a bit short-sighted. We Aspies have a habit of reacting only to our experiences without taking others' feelings into account. When we complain about what feels like an inconvenience, we may fail to notice that someone's actually done something nice for us. The "reward" for being kind to us should be a genuine "thank-you"; it should *not* be an "it's-all-about-me" tirade.

The thing is that Aspies are a little more self-referenced than your average NT. That is to say that it is harder for us to step outside our own thoughts and experiences. We are a little more stuck in our heads, our own interests, our own lives. In fact, if you pay attention, we tend to use the word "I" rather often. To other people, that looks like arrogance or self-centeredness. It's not. Self-centered and arrogant mean you think you are more important than others. That's not you. Or me. Usually, our trouble is that we have to be reminded (or learn to remember) to step outside of our own thoughts in the first place.

No guilt trip. I totally get it. We're not ungrateful, we're intensely absorbed. If I have a book in my hands (which now means all the time since e-reader apps), the last thing I want to do is…well, anything. I'm content in my own world. But, the fact is that my own little world isn't the world that is going to pay me, love me, feed me or shelter me. If we want to be included, liked, hired, or invited to anything or by anyone, then learning how and when to say a sincere thank-you is an absolute must. A "non-optional social convention." Why?

Really good thank-yous are how we show others that:

- We understand they've CHOSEN to be kind to us.
- We recognize that their resources (money, time, etc.) could be spent elsewhere.
- We appreciate that we matter to them.

When we don't thank others (even if it's just because we forget) NTs think:

- We don't care about what was given to or done for us.
- We're self-centered.
- We don't appreciate or care about the gift or the giver.

And the result? Friends decide we're not really worth any more of their energy. They kick us out of groups and just avoid us altogether. Family members and teachers will feel unimportant, and aren't too willing to help out again. Putting it straight: we're on our own.

What started off as a little "thank-you" turns out to be pretty big stuff, after all. So, let's just break down these hard-to-figure-out expectations into three little steps:

Notice, Tell, Thank

First, **notice** when someone spends time with or money on you. They didn't have to. It was a choice they made because they value you.

Second, **tell** them a specific feeling that their fondness gave you. *That feeling* was the REAL gift. Stumped on what to say? Try one of these words for starters:

"I felt (insert feeling word) about/because/when (their behavior)."

Example: **"I felt glad when you invited me."**

Better than "Happy"	Better than "Good"	Better than "Nice"
lucky	comfortable	included
important	encouraged	confident
glad	bright	proud
thankful	reassured	excited

Asperguy note: Learning how to identify your feelings is just as important for you, especially as you start dating and dealing with girls (we just talk about that stuff more, and we like it when guys actually admit they HAVE feelings). But, you're probably not going to want to get quite so "touchy feely" with other guys. That's another one of those "unwritten" lines that may make people uncomfortable if you cross it. So, guy-to-guy, you can change the "tell" part of the strategy to something like this:

> **"It was cool of you to (what they did)."**

> Example: **"It was cool of you to invite me to the party."**

Third, **thank** them in words and in actions. Remember that just because you FEEL grateful or happy on the inside, unless you speak up, no one else knows what you are thinking. You have to really spell it out for others to understand:

> **"Thanks for (the gift or action)."**

> Finish up with: **"Thanks for including me."**

The Potty Rule

Let's say someone recorded your favorite show, did a household chore for you, or saved you a seat at lunch. Maybe the person gave you some good advice or stuck up for you when you needed it. That person has gone out of his way to keep you in his life or make you feel happy. Maybe your mom spent money on an activity you like instead of on something for herself. These are the little things that matter a lot overall.

Because those kindnesses are sort of quiet ways of saying "I like you," they can be hard to miss. My family came up with a "thank-you" guide based on (just work with me here) a kids' potty-training show. In the program, one stuffed bear advised another, "Whenever you think you might have to go, you probably do." And you know what I've discovered? The potty-training rule works for a lot of things. "Thank-yous" being one.

Whenever you *think* you should say THANK YOU, you probably should.

The hard truth is that **failing to recognize others' words or actions makes us seem unappreciative**. Which is totally untrue. So take the time to look around and try to NOTICE who and what made your day a little nicer, a little easier. And if you *think* maybe you should say thank you, you probably should. You can never go wrong. Just try leaving a "trail of little sparks of gratitude" every day and "you will be surprised how they will set small flames of friendship" all around you (Carnegie 1936, p.23).

Don't worry, even with your new "thank-you radar" tuned in, you may still "miss" sometimes. It's OK. That's when the other two big words come in handy: "I'm sorry." Still, more often than not, the "potty-training" rule works. And you'll be right. It was worth a thank-you, after all.

3

So You Noticed a Kindness

The Technicalities of Thank You

Need-to-Knows

- "Thank-Yous" come in different levels, and NTs will expect you to know which kind is right for each situation.

- Sometimes, saying "thank you" is enough. Other times, more is expected.

- "Notice, Tell, Thank" works in written thank-yous as well.

- Written thank-yous can be sent as handwritten notes, e-cards and digital photo cards, or emails, depending on the type of note and who is receiving it.

- Thank-you gifts are the way to go when someone does something extra special for you.

- Never let your thank-you gift outshine the original gift.

Asperkid Logic

Whether it's another kid or your little brother, your dad or the school janitor, everyone deserves to be acknowledged for the nice things they do. That's called "reciprocity," and the kind of "gift" it requires of you is really more of your heart than from your wallet. You wouldn't give someone a gift just because they bought you a birthday present. And you don't have to go wash your mom's clothes because she did yours. Like in math, where reciprocal fractions are sort of reverse images of one another, reciprocity in social relationships is the yin to the yang, the reflection to the original—responding to one positive action with another positive action, rewarding one kindness with another.

Remember "NTT: Notice, Tell, Thank"? OK, so let's say you have "noticed" a kindness. Good start. But showing appreciation does take effort and it does take time. That's kind of the point. Acknowledging another person's kindness with your own time, words or service says that you know his or her time is as valuable as your own.

Mom did your laundry and then asked you to please put it away. You may be disappointed at having to spend your free time hanging up shirts, sure. But your mom probably didn't have herself a party while moving your wet underwear from the washer to the dryer. I'll bet she, too, could've found something more fun to do with her time—but out of love, she spent her time on you. Dreading writing thank-you notes after your birthday party? True, it may not be the most exciting thing to do. Then again, your friend might've bought a new gaming cartridge or model set with the money he spent on your gift.

NTT Practice

Time to NTT them. (And yes, you can change up the order if you want—NTT, TNT, whatever works. No worries.) For example, you might say:

> "Dad, you recorded *Monster Bug Wars* (**NOTICE**)! I'm really happy you thought of doing that for me (**TELL**). Thanks a lot (**THANKS**)."

> OR

> "Hey, Jenna, that was cool how you waited for me before music class (**NOTICE**). Thanks. I was so glad to have a friend to walk with (**THANKS** and **TELL**)."

Thank You—Turned Up a Notch

OK, you've got that NTT stuff down. Good, because spoken thank-yous cover most situations. However, when someone gives you a gift of any value or does something thoughtful that really impacts your life in a positive way, it's time to turn your appreciation up a notch and write a thank-you note.

With a few exceptions, the social "rules" still say handwritten, not typed, is expected. That takes more time, for sure, which is the point. By putting more effort into writing out your thank-you, you show how important the gift or deed was.

When is a Written Thank-You Expected?

Generally, the NT rules are that you write your thanks out when:

- You've been given a present, and the gift-giver isn't there to thank face-to-face; by writing a note, you assure the person her gift arrived safely, that you appreciated it and the effort she made to have it delivered to you.

- You've been given a gift for a celebration—like a birthday, graduation or religious celebration. (One exception: if you and the giver live in the same home, you don't have to write a note, but you DO need to say a specific, sincere thank-you for the gift.)

- You've been the guest of honor at a party.

- You've stayed at someone's home for a few nights (maybe your parents were on a trip) or for a special visit away from home (to your grandparents, a cousin or a long-distance friend). Their warm hospitality—food, space and entertainment— was a big gift!

- You've benefited from someone's talent (a friend helped redecorate your room) or time (a neighbor fed your pet rabbit while you were out of town).

- You've had an interview—for a job or for school admission. The employer or admissions officer took valuable time from other duties to meet with you and give your application consideration.

But What Do I Say?

A solid thank-you note is really just a written out version of the "NTT" rule. Just promise me you're going to use that Aspie brain to imagine up better adjectives to describe the gift or your feelings than: good, nice or fine. You can do sooooo much better!

1. **Notice:** why you are writing—you are saying thank you! Specifically name the gift or action for which you are thankful. *Exception Alert!* If the gift was money (cash, gift card, check, whatever), use the words "your generous gift" instead of specifying an amount, which isn't really important and is impolite to mention.

2. **Tell:** how you will use it and how nice it feels to be cared about, thought of, listened to, included, etc. Be positive no matter what. If you really *do* love the gift, say so. Like, "That book may become my new favorite! It's great!"

On the other hand, you can always find something nice to say, even if you don't like the present. Great-Aunt Mildred sent hot pink stretch pants that you wouldn't wear EVER? No problem. Try, "The color is a real crowd-stopper—so bright and lively." It's honest and, after all, it is the sentiment behind the gift that matters.

Oh, and if you've been given cash, etc., give an idea of how you will spend or save it. For example, "Your generous gift will really help me save up for a new laptop."

3. **Thank:** the other person again before signing off. And you're done!

Anything missing? Yes! A thank-you note is about the gift, not about you. Leave newsy tidbits for the next time you chat.

A Matter of Time
Thank-you notes should be written as soon as possible. BUT no matter how late your thank-you note, it's always true—better late than never. Apologize for the delay and write it anyway!

Email or Snail Mail?
Personal notes should really be handwritten; try your best to be neat, but don't worry about how perfect your handwriting is or isn't. It's the effort you are putting in that counts. However, if having to handwrite a note is obstacle enough to make you throw your hands up and scrap the whole thing, you do have some fun twenty-first century options:

- **E-cards:** they are fun and fast.
- **Apps and programs:** lots of desktop computers have postcard/stationery functions built right in, which is really fun because you can insert photos of the gift being used, or of you and the giver; similarly, smartphone and tablet apps make saying thank-you creative and easy—point, click and drag your way into instant postcards or greeting cards that are ACTUALLY posted and mailed for you.

Formal thank-yous (job or college interview, etc.): If an email address is listed on someone's business card, or if someone from the business has emailed you, then yes, it's alright to send a carefully worded, carefully proofread email. Just be sure you spellcheck it (sending anything misspelled digitally looks lazy, since the computer can help do the proofing for you) and keep clear of any "signature" quotations after your name. If you can't decide how to reach them, you can NEVER go wrong by handwriting a note.

I Still Need Help!

Seriously, no sweat. Getting started on the note is the hardest part. Check out the Resources List at the back of this book for my favorite "manners" guides, tweets and podcasts that will help you say whatever you want or need to without any worries about finding the right words.

One Step Further: The Thank-You Gift

There are occasions when, beyond even a note, you really ought to have an actual "thank-you gift" ready. Teachers, coaches, scouting leaders. Maybe someone gave you a big break. Anyone who devotes a large chunk of time to you would really like to know that he or she has made a difference. And in these cases, you can go that extra bit with a gift of your own.

Personally, I have a "treasure box" in my closet where I keep little stuffed animals, poems, photos and mementos given to me by my students. These trinkets are some of the most precious things I have, because they remind me that I mattered to these kids.

How Much is Too Much?

Just when this all seemed pretty logical and laid out, I have to warn you of a hidden social pitfall. Overkill. And this, for us Aspies, is a biggie. We often go big or go broke, when somewhere in the middle is the best answer.

You see, an over-the-top thank-you gift or note in return for a small favor might actually embarrass the recipient. Instead of thinking kindly of you, the person may see you as desperate or clingy, and avoid or joke about you. Complete backfire. In an episode of the old TV show, *Seinfeld*, the character named Elaine bought her friend a cup of coffee; he, then, bought her a coffeemaker as a thank you. His much more expensive, substantial thank-you was so out of proportion that it created enough confusion to fuel a thirty-minute sitcom. Why?

The thank-you should always be less fancy and less expensive than the original gift or deed (otherwise it becomes a sort of weird, never-ending competition). Let the other person's gift shine without stealing the spotlight.

Good Sense and Pink Pants

As Aspies, we're going to make mistakes speaking "Social-ease." It's a given. We're not natives to these rules, and from time to time, every Aspie is going to blow it. But at least with all of these particulars in your back pocket, you're a lot less likely to get tripped up on the small, technical stuff. Don't try to memorize it all—come back and check when you need to. After all, Asperkids are naturals at following rules that make good, logical sense. And when you get to the bottom of it, this whole "thank-you" rule makes good sense. It is important to stop what we are doing long enough to acknowledge when other people treat us well (especially if we want them to keep treating us well!). And yes, that even goes for Great-Aunt Mildred…just cross your fingers that next time she picks out something besides hot pink stretch pants.

Quotealicious

IT MAY NOT TURN OUT THE WAY YOU PLANNED. IT MAY TURN OUT BETTER.

You are the only you there ever has been, or is, or will be. Be the you-iest you you can be.

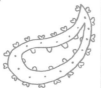

Pick yourself up. Dust yourself off. Repeat.

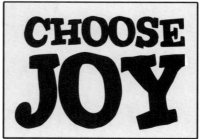

CHOOSE JOY

- 4 -

I'm Sorry

The Hardest Words to Say

Need-to-Knows

- "I'm sorry" don't have to be the hardest words to say. But they are some of the most important.
- Apologies don't make one person a winner and the other a loser.
- A good apology says what went wrong, which feelings got hurt, and what should've happened instead.
- One mistake does not a friendship break.
- Forgiving isn't the same as forgetting.

Asperkid Logic

You've probably heard that we Aspies see the world in black and white. Not as in old-TV-show-black-and-white, but as in up-or-down, in-or-out, all-or-nothing. People, however, are not that simple. Neither are the ways they get along. Which is why when somebody steps on somebody else's feelings—by accident or not—repair work has to be done if the two people are going to continue to get along.

In an either/or, right or wrong world, one side is the "winner" and the other is the "loser." No wonder Aspies can have such a tough time apologizing. Who wants to be the loser? Right? Wrong. **Apologizing doesn't mean someone is a loser, it means the relationship is more important than your ego.**

Why is Saying "Sorry" So Important?

Think of a good relationship as a balanced scale. Both sides are equal. When one person hurts the other, she essentially "steals" some of his happiness. The scale is lopsided. If that relationship is going to get back to a "balanced" place, she's going to have to make things right again. That's the apology. And while no one likes to apologize, I've learned the secret behind this rule: saying you are sorry isn't a sign that you are weak or the "loser." Actually, just the opposite is true.

Apologies aren't easy because they're not supposed to be. Saying sorry is meant to make us feel awkward. Maybe even nervous or rattled. That's why, when done right, apologies are so powerful. It's uncomfortable to admit that we've hurt someone's feelings. It's also uncomfortable to "hold the pillow" and really face our less-than-best-selves head-on. **We Aspies aren't worth less than anyone else, but we're not worth more either.**

And Now…A Story from "This is My Aspie Life"

It was mid-afternoon when my mom pulled into the parking lot. She was a little bit late in arriving to pick a friend and me up from a shopping trip because she'd been at the hair salon. Things had apparently not gone as they usually did, and when she drove up, I should've noticed two things right away: her face was flushed and her voice sounded funny. But I didn't notice. I was too caught up in having a friend by my side. I don't know what happened to my mom at the salon, but she muttered something to us about not being happy with the stylist or the cut. And yes, it really did look terrible.

Without thinking, I made some wisecrack like, "I can see why you're mad!" and giggled to my friend. I was trying to be funny and cool, I guess. Trying to impress her (really dumb move). You know, I can't even remember who that girl was now. But I can remember my mom's reaction. She started crying. It never even occurred to me that she could feel embarrassed like I did when kids laughed at me. Yet obviously, she did.

Sometimes we can tell that we've done something wrong but aren't sure what. Other times, like this awful moment, we just totally and completely blow it. Maybe those apologies should be the easiest—there was no doubt about who was wrong in this case. But I didn't want to be the loser. And I was really, really ashamed. My pride got in the way of making things right. As often as I'd been made fun of, I'd just done the same to my poor mom. So I argued that she was overreacting. That I hadn't meant any harm. But the whole time, I knew it was me.

Here's the thing: saying and being sorry is really, really important. **We have to feel safe with the people who are close to us. We have to know that they care about how we feel and are willing to admit their mistakes. But it's also important for them to feel safe with us.** If we can't or don't take responsibility for things we do wrong, we make others feel that they can't trust us…which is not going to win us any friends.

A really good apology shows that you value *making* **things right more than you value** *being* **right.**

A *Good* Apology?

A good apology needs the right place and the right words to have the right effect.

What's the Right Place?

Alone. Whatever is wrong is between you and another person and should stay that way. Ask to speak in private and in person (definitely avoid texting or online wall posts).

What's the Right Way?

For an apology to mean something, you have to understand what you did and why you're saying you are sorry. In other words, you have to see (though not necessarily agree with) the other person's point of view.

Uh-oh. Wait. That whole understanding someone else's feelings thing? That's empathy, right? Right. **Aspie pitfall alert!** Because we have a harder time interpreting body language or tone of voice, Aspies often don't even realize we've done something hurtful. That makes it really hard to take responsibility for a mistake or ask for forgiveness.

If you think someone is upset with you, but don't know why, ask. You may feel scared of the answer; you may not even agree with it. But NOT knowing (or pretending not to know) why the other person is hurt doesn't make the problem go away—it only makes it worse. So does being too scared or too proud to apologize. Don't be afraid to step up and ask to talk.

If you do see that you've made a mistake, do something about it. After all, if you were driving a car and realized you'd missed your highway exit, would you just keep driving? No. You'd pull off, turn around and get back on the right road. That's what you need to do with people, too.

In one of my favorite books, *All I Really Need To Know I Learned in Kindergarten* (Fulghum 2004), little kids remind us that we learned all the important stuff a long time ago. Among the lessons they share are: "Play fair…Clean up your own mess," and, "Say you're sorry when you hurt somebody." If little kids can do this, so can we.

The Trusty Apology Formula

1. Say, **"I'm sorry."** Own it. Don't make any excuses or try to wriggle out of it. You are here to make things right.

2. Now's when you fill in the part about **what you did**. Be as clear and particular as you can be—that's how the other person knows you listened and heard his version of events.

3. Bonus points! How might you feel if the roles were reversed? There's a pretty good chance that's **what he's feeling** now. Say so.

4. Say that **you won't do it again**. And mean it. Sorry is as sorry does. If you say you won't repeat an offense, but keep doing the same thing over and again, you aren't really sorry.

5. Ask for **forgiveness**. Forgiveness doesn't mean the mistake is forgotten or even that the hurt is gone—that takes time. Forgiveness means that he understands and believes you are truly sorry.

An example (that I wish I'd have used!) might go like this:

"Mom, I'm sorry I made fun of your haircut and maybe made you feel embarrassed, too. I won't tease you again. Will you please forgive me?"

On the flip side, if someone cares enough about you to offer a sincere apology, accept it. Remember the dangers of black-and-white, all-or-nothing thinking:

One mistake does not a friendship break.

You mess up, I mess up. An occasional blunder doesn't mean we're completely disposable (thank goodness!).

Sometimes "I'm Sorry" Doesn't Cut It

There are a few special situations where "I'm sorry" is not enough to keep you around:

- If any relationship involves you **having to say sorry often**, it's probably not a very healthy one to be in.

- If someone asks for forgiveness, but then **continues to hurt you, that's not really being sorry**, no matter how hard they claim to be "trying." Forgiving isn't the same as forgetting or being someone's doormat.

- Remember the rule about no excuses? If another person apologizes but then finds a way to blame you for the mistake he or she made, that's a no-go. **You are never responsible for someone else choosing to hurt you. Ever.**

- And last, take this from someone who has been there: no one—ever, for any reason—gets to hurt you or **make you feel afraid**. No apology covers that. No excuses or explanations. Period.

Making friends isn't nearly as hard as keeping them, I have found. One takes a few conversation starters or a common interest. The other takes effort, time, and a lot of sustained attention. In fact, in a lot of cases, you only know you've made a true friend once you've had a rough patch and worked your way back through it together. It takes a big person to say those two very little—very powerful—words, "I'm sorry." It takes another to hear them and accept them. Then, once it's done, let it be done. Agree to put the whole deal behind you and move on to a better tomorrow.

5

The "Perseverance" of "Perserverance"

Being Right vs. Being Included

Need-to-Knows

- Being right isn't always the most important thing, even when it feels that way.
- How you correct an error (humbly, in private) is as important as whether you correct it.
- Peers don't like to be corrected by one another.

- Unless there's danger, never correct an adult or authority figure.

- Knowing when, how or if you should point out someone's mistake isn't easy, but it is doable.

Asperkid Logic

For Aspies, words have to be accurate. Facts have to be true. Or valid. Or at least not wrong. Listening to anything less is like nails on a chalkboard or the sound of styrofoam blocks rubbing together. It's grating and almost impossible to ignore.

There was an uncle in the family who had a collection of Hummels: collectable ceramic figurines that were awfully popular in the 1950s and 1960s. Mostly, they are little Germanic kids in kerchiefs and scarves and clogs...and they are NOT playthings. Ask any kid who has ever visited a house where someone collects Hummels, and they know. You don't touch the Hummels.

Well, Uncle Bob had Hummels. They lined his high shelves, perfectly arranged for display, yet most definitely out of reach. Only they weren't high enough. Because when the kids would visit, someone always snuck away to the collection, reached up... and turned around one Hummel. Just to mess with him. Just one, little, tiny thing off—among the otherwise meticulously arranged ceramic children—would be as irritating as that little tag in the neck of your new shirt.

To Aspies, getting things right isn't about being the one who is right, it's about having things as they should be.

Neurotypicals don't really get that. On their end, they see us breaking all sorts of other social rules in pursuit of the highest Aspie rule of all—truth. And so, if you correct a teacher who asks you to put away your coat and you reply that you don't have a coat, you have a rain jacket, she is not going to care that, in fact, you are correct. She's going to notice (as are the kids around you) that you have just simultaneously broken two social rules—(1) Not correcting people in front of others, and (2) Not correcting an elder. Big no-no's. So you, my friend, are in trouble. Oh...and the kids who heard the conversation are probably thinking that you are trying to embarrass the teacher—probably also not a big win.

Sometimes, the world feels like it just goes a million miles wrong in an instant. You were talking about rain jackets and suddenly everyone's mad at you. When did THAT happen?

The Lesson of the Whiteboard

Last week, I was at the karate studio near our house. They are awesome instructors with a great dedication to helping kids grow into amazing people, not just into black-belts. One of the ways they do that is by highlighting a character word each week. This particular week the word happened to be "perseverance." On every whiteboard in the room, they'd written "perseverance" in bright markers. Bold, fluorescent, "perseverance." Only I noticed a blaring mistake. Instead of "perserverance," they'd written "perseverance."

Of course, they meant stick-to-it-ive-ness. But when talking "Aspie," perseverance usually means "obsession." One idea—stuck in your head—repeating over and over. And over. And over.

And there I was, perseverating on the word perseverance. I couldn't pay attention to the lesson, or the instructors. All I could think about was that "perserverance" was written (everywhere I looked) as "perseverance."

This wasn't the first time that had happened. A couple of months ago, the cycle of character words had been in the same spot, and once again, they had misspelled "perserverance." Without really thinking about it, I'd blurted out to the instructors (in front of spectators and a class) that they'd made a mistake and misspelled the word of the week.

In all fairness, they were way nicer than they needed to be. I'm pretty sure the teacher blushed—because in pointing out a blunder, I had, albeit unintentionally, made him feel dumb for making a lame spelling error. He laughed it off, and I (trying hard to stuff my words back into my mouth) tried to blow it off by making a lame joke about being a spelling fanatic. AWK-WARD.

That's kind of the way this Aspies-must-be-accurate-about-all-things trouble goes down. We Aspies are never going to escape our urgent need for precision. That's OK. Actually, it's more than OK. It's part of what makes our minds special and able to achieve the levels of intense analysis that allowed Marie Curie to discover radium or Mozart to compose with such genius.

It's just that the karate studio is not the Curies' lab. And the school lunchroom is not Mozart's study.

If we want the neurotypical world to react positively to us, we have to learn the secret rules for how and when to make corrections. This, like everything else I'm telling you, I have learned from first NOT knowing the rules.

Basically, you have to look at the payoff. It feels good to fix an error. Like cracking a knuckle or taking a deep breath. Ah, that's better. But that's only true for the one who did the fixing. Think about it: if someone points out your social mistakes frequently, or when others are watching, how do you feel? Probably annoyed and embarrassed at the very least.

How You Correct an Error is at Least as Important as Whether You Correct It

What are you doing right now? You're reading a book that is, well, talking about some of our common Aspie pitfalls. You can handle this because I am telling you privately (well, yes, it's a book, but you ARE reading my words, not having them read TO you). Furthermore, the prospect of feeling better about yourself, having more friends, dates, getting along with adults, is worth a little discomfort.

It's almost like a math equation. Which is greater, the importance of making a particular correction right away OR holding on long enough to do something else about it? Is your goal to have things be "right" or to start a fight? We Aspies operate on logic most of the time. The rest of the world doesn't. Out there, pride, emotion and reputations rule. So, be careful. A famous book says the first principle to getting along with others is "don't criticize, condemn or complain" (Carnegie 1936, p.17). But criticism is exactly how your correction may sound to others' ears.

And that's a powerful and dangerous thing—even if you don't mean it to be. Challenging another person usually hurts his pride and makes him feel embarrassed or dumb. Once that happens, the result is almost NEVER graceful acceptance or change for the better; it's feelings of anger and resentment toward you. The more you try to prove someone wrong, the more he's likely to argue he is right.

In some cases, "correct it now" does win. Before your lab partner dumps an explosive into the Bunsen burner, yes—now is the time to stop her. Emergencies notwithstanding, though, here are some guidelines to help figure out when/whether it is worth making a correction:

The If's, When's and How's
Evaluate: Can It Wait?

- Is he/she busy right now? Too busy to really listen?
- Is he/she in front of other people?
- Does the "error" change the main idea, or is it just a detail?
- Does an approximation *have* to be specific to get the general point across (i.e. that a trip is thirteen minutes long, not ten)?
- Is anyone going to be harmed by letting it be wrong?

If you can, hold on until you think it through some more. You can even write down what you want to say if you really need to "get it out" immediately…like a pressure release.

Privacy, Please

No one likes to be corrected in front of other people. When I was a kid, there was nothing worse than if my mom punished me in front of other people. I couldn't even hear her point; I was too busy being mortified. Same goes. **When you correct someone in front of a crowd, they don't listen, they react (and not well, usually). If your intention is really just to correct a mistake and not to embarrass the person who made it, wait until you are alone.**

Online, Too

Facebook, Twitter, whatever. That's public, too. Even an email or text can easily be forwarded.

Down, Yes, Across, Maybe, Up, No Way

You can kindly correct someone over whom you have control or influence (like babysitting, coaching or tutoring). Only correct a peer if you HAVE to—they won't like it (that's when you're going to hear, "You're not the boss of me!"). And never, ever, ever, correct an elder or an authority figure. They may be wrong and you may be right, but unless safety demands it, correcting "up" is just rude.

Fact or Opinion?

Facts can be verified. 2+2=4. Always. Opinions vary. They can be supported—but they can also be argued. Be sure that you're correcting a FACT only. Your opinion, just like anyone else's, is not absolute.

Watch the Language

Statements that begin with, "I may have noticed" or "I think maybe" are a lot less aggressive than "You're wrong." Make your observation **about the fact, not the person**.

Just Let It Go

Sometimes, there is a bigger reward for leaving a mistake alone, no matter how uncomfortable it feels to us Aspies. If you know a teacher meant "anecdote" when he said "antidote," but he's already begun the story, don't bother to bring the attention back your way. It's not worth it, and you may learn something interesting if you can refocus on the larger point being made.

Leaving Well Enough Alone

With practice, it gets easier to see the payoff for leaving well enough alone. There are times when we are all glad not to have our less-than-best moments pointed out.

Have patience if this takes some time to figure out. Learning when, if, or how to right a wrong is something that a whole lot of adults (Aspies and otherwise) still have trouble with.

Which leads us back to me at the karate studio, where life had suddenly handed me a "do over." I'm a big believer that mistakes are only mistakes if we don't learn from them. So I was bound and determined to learn from mine.

That dang perseverance was perseverating, I promise you. Same word, same misspelling. I couldn't believe it! Fate was dangling this perseverating perseveration in front of me, daring me to speak up. But this time, I recognized the trap, and held my tongue. Seated in the back of the studio gallery, I pulled out my phone and texted a friend (pressure release!), making fun of my own silly preoccupation with the mistake.

And then, absolute poetic justice.

You see, the one guideline I didn't mention above was the most important of all:

Before you speak up, be sure you are right.

As I texted, my spellcheck rebelled. What was this? I went to my dictionary app. WHAT?!

Ahem. "Perserverance," it seems, is not a word at all. Here I am, a published author, a grammar lover, a former English teacher, and I have apparently been both mispronouncing and misspelling persevere as "perservere" (and, therefore, any forms of the word) my entire life long.

Ah, humility. In the end, we all learned a lesson. I learned that there is no "r" in the middle of a word I have been using for ages. And the karate students learned about never giving up, even if they are tired or frustrated or (gulp) embarrassed… something a lot more important than a spelling error, especially a nonexistent spelling error. Sometimes, I guess, it just takes some "perseverance" to know when to speak up and when to be awfully glad we've let it go.

6

Perfectly Imperfect

Congratulations, You're Human

Need-to-Knows

- Wanting to be excellent is good. Wanting to improve is great. Wanting to be perfect is arrogant.

- Perfectionism makes any amount of success worthless compared to a single failure.

- Our perfectionism comes across to other people as annoying, smug superiority.

- Other people want to be able to relate to you. No one can relate to "perfect."

Asperkid Logic

Everyone likes to feel like a success. That's pretty much a no-brainer. After all, who wakes up in the morning and says, "I can't wait to fail at everything I try today!" Nobody. We all want to feel proud, smart, attractive, important. And some people put on quite a show convincing the world of just how amazing they are. Oddly, though, the people who seem most convinced of their fabulousness are usually those who are the least convinced of it themselves.

Still, wanting to improve any part of our lives is a good thing. It can help us strengthen friendships, do better at school, even get healthier. That's wonderful. The trouble is when "better" stops being the goal, and "perfect" takes its place. Gradually, we concentrate only on what we do wrong, no matter how much we do right. It's like being a famous singer, performing onstage in front of thousands of cheering fans—and all you can see is the one grumpy kid frowning from the back row. The thousands of other fans screaming their lungs out are powerless and valueless, compared with that single downer. **When perfection is the goal, we will always fail.** And, sadly, we allow all of our power, all of our worth to be squelched by one, puny blemish.

That's our Aspie black-and-white, all-or-nothing thinking. It makes some situations easier and less messy, but all-in-all, it does lead us to be a lot harder on ourselves than we should be. Partly, that's because we're awfully afraid of failure. Most people are, but we seem to corner the market. Understandable, really. We've usually had more than our fair share of unexpectedly "messing up" in the NT world, leading to more than our fair share of teasing, rejection and insults. Really, it's no wonder we're so scared of blowing it! Who wants more of that? Add the creeping awareness that we can't control very much in the world, and we're in for a full-blown freakout. Trust me, people, I've been there.

So You Want to Argue With Universal Laws...

My mom was a pretty average student. According to her, if she did really well on a test, it was a celebration, and if she didn't, it wasn't the end of the world. Then there was me—self-confessed major perfectionist. If I smeared the ink on my homework, I rewrote the entire thing. I couldn't even count sheep to get to sleep—know why? I got way too stressed as I counted down from 100…every number mentally translated into a possibly-less-than-perfect grade. 98? "Argh?!" I would cringe, "Where did I go wrong?"

I know, I know. Kind of annoying, right? Not to mention ulcer-causing. But I'll bet you are equally hard on yourself—perfectionism is a lot easier to recognize in another person. And Aspies are notorious perfectionists. We see the world and ourselves as right or wrong, all or nothing. Then, we beat ourselves up in the process—because **trying to be perfect is the most imperfect goal imaginable**. It's not achievable. It doesn't exist. It's like insisting you will be a success only if you become the next Santa Claus. Not going to happen, folks. If that's the only thing that will make you happy, you might as well decide to live a life of misery now.

On the other hand, **imperfection is completely natural**. Ever hear of Brownian movement? It's the imperceptible, random movement of the tiniest microscopic particles. Even when things look "perfectly" calm and smooth, there's actually a whole mess of chaotic, haphazard jiggling going on. That's just the way the universe works: thermodynamic laws say so. It's entropy, or naturally occurring disorder. Just try and argue why you (or we) are above universal laws, and I guarantee you'll come up stumped. Although we Aspies are, in many ways, very different than the NTs around us, we are also the same in one important way: **every mortal person that has ever existed—Aspie or NT—is imperfect and always will be**. Depressed? Don't be. You're in good company. Einstein. Gandhi. Mother Teresa. Each and every one was imperfect, too. So be careful of the all-or-nothing trap. Imperfection doesn't mean utter failure.

Sabotage

Which brings us to another way perfectionism sabotages us. It turns out that in our quest to be perfect and avoid public humiliation, we end up being incredibly irritating as well. Perfect.

"Kids like you used to make me furious," my mom told me once, much to my surprise. Earlier that day, I'd gotten a test back on which I'd made a 96 percent. Most people, I now understand, would have killed for a 96. That's a totally solid "A" or "excellent" grade. But not me. I was a wreck. In class, my face had fallen, and all I could think about was the stupid mistake I'd made on one lousy question that I should've gotten right in the first place. Now, hours later, I was still upset.

What never occurred to me was how that reaction looked to other kids. Or what I was doing to myself in the process.

Don't get me wrong—it's good to want to be excellent. It's great to want to improve. It's the whole "how you handle yourself" bit that's tough, especially if you're not really thinking about how you come off to the people around you. **Perfectionism is really just a nicer-sounding word for arrogance.** It's the belief or expectation that we should be above making mistakes. Be better or more special than everyone else around us. Basically, that we are above being human. And that, I tell you from personal experience, is not going make people invite you to sit at their lunch tables.

Here is what I didn't realize back in high school: to most kids, my worst grade was better than their best. So my complaining was sort of a high school version of Marie Antoinette. "Let them eat cake" and all. I had meant to criticize myself. But others were, of course, watching. Without even thinking about it, I had sent the condescending message that I believed myself superior to everyone in the room. I'd been disappointed in myself—but from any other person's perspective, I was insulting them, too. My pouting perfectionism didn't just hurt my own self-esteem. It also made other people feel lousy about themselves, then jealous of and completely irritated by me. Meaning, of course, that they would treat me as if I were vain and self-centered. Which, not meaning to be, I guess I was.

The weird flip side is that if a friend had gotten an "A" on a test, I would have congratulated her. Been proud of her. And I should have been proud of me. Being smart, or kind, or fast, or creative is something people admire. Being annoyingly perfect (or even worse, thinking or acting as if you are) is, well, annoying.

The Tightrope and the Shoebox

Life, it turns out, is a bit like a tightrope act at the circus. You are the aerialist, balancing on a skinny little wire—and you think everyone is there to watch you glide amazingly, perfectly from one end to the other. But the secret is…that isn't at all what the world wants. The world loves to watch arrogant people fail and fall. Just check the tabloid papers.

To win the crowd's love, people need to see us bobble on life's tightrope. Be relatable. Be imperfectly human. And you know what? *We* need those moments to remind ourselves of our human-ness. And to make everyone around gasp with us and cheer us on.

Really, no one else cares about your success or failure as much as you think they do—it's your reaction they will notice. Do you freak out like I did? Will you take yourself too seriously (which translates as: I am sooo much better than you)? Or will you just be happily, humbly human like everyone else? Imperfect, but real. If you would congratulate a friend had he accomplished what you have, then congratulate yourself. **Sometimes good enough IS good enough.**

Imagine putting any mistakes into a shoebox, shutting the lid, and placing it on a high closet shelf. It's still there, if you really need to revisit it. But it's not in your face. Now, find a specific thing you did well—like you played great defense in the second half or you completely nailed that essay question—own it, and move on. You'll like yourself a lot more for it, and so will the people around you.

7

But I Wasn't Laughing

Laughing with You vs. Laughing at You

Need-to-Knows

- It can be hard to tell the difference between playful teasing, mean teasing and accidental hurts.

- Aspies tend to take ourselves super-seriously. That's not the same as being "too sensitive."

- Ask yourself: Do I trust the person who is teasing me? Would they really want to hurt me? Perhaps we're miscommunicating.

Asperkid Logic

I was six years old, I think. We were lined up in a row facing the mirrored wall and a bevy of visitors in folding chairs. It was Parents' Observation Day at Skip Randall Dance School, and when the music began, we all did our best to show off our new tap routine. When we got to the part when we wagged our fingers and popped our hips like sassy little ladies, the whole audience giggled adoringly. "How cute!" they all laughed. Only I didn't want to be cute and funny. We were supposed to look grown-up! I was insulted and embarrassed…and MAD. And I started crying. Later, my mom explained that the grown-ups weren't laughing AT us, they had thought we were so precious that they were laughing WITH us.

I looked her straight in the eye and said, "But I wasn't laughing."

Fast-forward to middle school. I was on an overnight hotel trip with my dance company in New York City. Out of the dozen or so girls, I was the youngest by a few years. I was also the best dancer…something which hadn't won me a lot of friends within the group.

The morning of the dance competition, I got into the shower. A minute or two later, the bathroom door opened—and a huge bucket of ice water came raining down over the shower curtain onto my head. The door slammed, and shrieks of laughter echoed from the bedroom. Absolutely alone—and shivering—I sat down on the tiles. I decided not to say a thing about it until I saw my parents later…when I did, their answer was that I was being too sensitive. The girls were probably just kidding around with me.

But I hadn't been kidding around.

Laughing with You vs. Laughing at You

We Aspies have a particularly hard time reading body language and tone of voice. Which is, I will admit, a total bummer for us, as reports say that anywhere between 55 and 80 percent of all communication is nonverbal. That's how much of the picture we may be missing in any face-to-face meeting.

It's no wonder that two things seem to happen as a result:

1. **We learn to take ourselves very seriously. Sometimes too seriously.** And sometimes we really do mistake friendly teasing or unintentionally hurt feelings for bullying. Why? When you can't tell clearly who is "for" you and who is "against" you, it doesn't take long before you walk around with your guard up—all the time. (That's what happened to me at the dance practice. The adults really WERE delighted by the bouncing bunch of adorable little girls. No one meant to insult us.)

2. **Other people don't trust us when we say we're being laughed at**—no one else heard or saw it. So, adults often assume, it didn't really happen. Or kids say we're too sensitive (no such thing exists) or can't take a joke. After a while, you wonder why you should bother defending yourself. (By the way—that's what happened in the hotel situation. I *was* being bullied but my parents thought I was just overreacting.)

Everyone makes bad jokes from time to time, or says things they wish they could take back. So, how *do* you distinguish playful teasing from accidental "ouches" or even hurtful teasing?

Ask Yourself this Question: Do I Trust the Person?

Do you? Do you feel safe being yourself with him or her? Is it your mom or a long-time friend, a teacher that you like or your favorite cousin…is this someone who loves you, who cares about your feelings? In other words, **based on everything you know about this person, do you think he or she would really WANT to put you down?** If you do trust the person—the hurt probably wasn't on purpose.

Even though our hurt is real, we Aspies often give meaning to actions or words that wasn't intended. Might this be a misunderstanding? It's possible that the person didn't realize he was getting too close to a sensitive topic. Or, it might help to remember that laughing at your own actions shows that you accept yourself as imperfect—like everyone else. **So, are *you* the joke? Or, if you can take a step back, is something you *did* or *said* actually quite funny?**

Teasing is even one way some NTs show affection. In my husband's family, teasing you means they like you—they trust you to know that they are kidding and mean no harm. That took me a while to get. It might be tough for you, too.

A Quiz

If you're not quite sure what someone's motivation is, take this little quiz:

Do I feel liked by this person (in general)?		
A. Yes	B. No	C. Not sure
Has this person hurt me before?		
A. No	B. Yes (on purpose)	C. Yes (but truly by accident)
Is the joke on a topic about which she knows I am insecure (e.g. weight) or passionate (e.g. vegetarianism)?		
A. Nope	B. Absolutely	C. Yes, but she doesn't know that
If I say, "I don't think that's very funny," and she realizes I'm serious, what would she say/do?		
A. "I'm really sorry."	B. Keeps laughing and teasing	C. Is perhaps surprised, but stops

If You Chose Mostly As: Playful Teasing

Odds are this is someone who cares about you and was trying to laugh WITH you—not AT you. This is a person who respects you and will stop if you say you don't like what's going on.

But—do ask yourself honestly if maybe you ARE taking yourself too seriously, because that just takes all the fun out of life. Is there really some truth to the teasing that is actually a bit funny? If yes, laugh. It takes the pressure off of trying to be so perfect, makes you seem more relatable, and will probably make for a great story ("Do you remember that time I was trying to talk to that girl and fell flat on my face? Literally?").

If You Chose Mostly Bs: Mean Teasing

Not funny. No way, no how. This isn't OK, and you're not being overly sensitive. You can take a joke, thank you, it's just that this isn't funny. Teasing that happens repeatedly, is about something you can't help (money, appearance) or really love (Star Wars, Harry Potter), is smoothed over with a fake "just joking!" or is meant to make you feel embarrassed or hurt is MEAN. And, it's not going to stop until you get an adult to step in. So don't wait.

If You Chose Mostly Cs: Accidental Ouch

Sometimes even our best friends mess up and say something that they shouldn't. In these cases, it's an "accidental ouch," teasing that isn't OK, but really wasn't meant to be hurtful—and will stop when you make it clear how you feel. So use an "I felt..." statement and expect a change. If it keeps happening, though, go back and see "mostly Bs."

Once you decide if this is a "with" you or "at" you kind of situation, read the rules in "Wedgies, Tattletales and Queen Bees" and/or "Through the Looking Glass" (mini-chapters 30 and 31). This is tricky stuff and takes practice. You've got allies—you just need to know where to look to find them.

Quotealicious

"Talking with quiet confidence will always beat screaming with obvious insecurity."

YOU CAN'T CONTROL HOW PEOPLE TREAT YOU. BUT. YOU ARE IN COMPLETE CONTROL OF HOW YOU REACT.

BE A FRIEND TO THYSELF AND OTHERS WILL BEFRIEND THEE

It takes courage to grow up and turn out to be who you really are.

8

Poof! You're Interesting!

Being Interesting by Being Interested

Need-to-Knows

- Everyone wants to feel heard and to know that they matter.
- Show what you know bit-by-bit so that everyone gets a chance to be heard.
- To be interesting to other people, you first have to be interested in them.

Asperkid Logic

The Oprah Winfrey Show first came to television sometime when I was in elementary school and for twenty-five years was a broadcast powerhouse. Whether you ever watched a single episode or not, you have to give some credit to a woman who was welcomed day after day, year after year, into living rooms around the world. When she ended the run in 2011, Ms. Winfrey summed up all that she had learned by saying:

> "I've talked to nearly 30,000 people on this show, and all 30,000 had one thing in common: They all wanted validation… They want to know: 'Do you see me? Do you hear me? Does what I say mean anything to you?'… The only time I made mistakes is when I didn't listen."

Asperkids are, in general, good talkers—at least when we get on those subjects we really love. Dinosaurs, space. Greek gods, super-heroes. Trains, animals. You know—the special interest that you could lose an entire day to without realizing an hour had slipped by. Well, in our "Aspie family," we have several special interests going at any one time. And I can tell you that someone who loves everything there is to love about mythology isn't necessarily interested in the differences between an allosaurus and a T Rex. The paleontologist isn't too keen on finding out every legend involving Athena, either, and neither is the junior Spiderman. So if we're not careful, dinnertime can sound like three running monologues—each Asperkid going on about his or her favorite topic without really involving the others.

It gets pretty noisy.

With all that talking, is anybody listening? Not really. Yet if you asked any of the kids, they would say that they were being friendly and upbeat. They were doing everything possible to be the kind of person everyone would want to know. Only they would be wrong.

Being Part of the Action—Not the Whole Game

Good conversations should be kind of like a well-matched tennis or volleyball point. You know how crowds watching the court look one way, then the other, then back, then over again? It's like a duet. One side doesn't overpower the other—both sides participate equally. That's how, in conversations and relationships too, everyone gets to feel part of the action.

We Aspies are great at remembering information—especially when it comes to our special interests. It's why Asperkids are often identified as "little professors" when we're very young. Only that's not entirely the compliment we might think it is. After all, we're darned proud of knowing every make of car or species of butterfly or whatever it is that fascinates you. And we should be! Our trouble is that we think the NT world is going to be impressed by that library of knowledge and want to hear everything we have to share—so we talk...and talk...and talk. We miss the signs that we are boring people, rather than interesting them, and are—even worse—coming off as "instructive" (a lovely word one counselor used to tell me that basically, I sounded like a know-it-all).

Nobody is going to like it if they think you are showing off.

So how do you manage to take part in—but not take over—a conversation if you do know a lot about the topic? Maybe even more than a teacher? Simple. You do it a little bit at a time. **We can spend all of our energy showing off everything we know to everyone, and we won't impress anybody. Or get people to like us.** Trust me on this one. I did it. And it's how I got the name "Dictionary Brain."

Talking more than listening. Talking about yourself. Your interests. Your experiences. Interrupting other people because you have an idea that just can't wait. That may be how you win trivia games (and I love my "Jeopardy!"), but it isn't how you make friends.

Instead, remind yourself:

• I know that I know what I know. Everyone else doesn't need to know it, too.

• Showing what I know a little bit at a time gives other people a chance to feel smart, too.

- I have to wait for the right moment to speak up—like when someone asks me a question or a teacher asks the whole class for an answer.

- I've got to be patient! Other people *will* eventually recognize that I know a lot about the topic.

- Because they've had a chance to participate, too, they'll be more eager to work with, talk with or hang out with me.

People Like People Who Make Them Feel Good about Themselves

Here is the not-very-nice-sounding but absolutely true fact: **"People are not interested in you. They are not interested in me. They are interested in themselves—morning, noon and after dinner"** (Carnegie 1936, p.34). It's nothing personal! It's just that, like Oprah said, everyone's greatest need is to feel noticed. Heard. To matter. That's true of you. Me. Everyone.

> **If you want to be interesting to other people, you must first take an interest in them.**

You don't do that by talking at them. You do that by **listening to them. Nothing you can say, no fact you can share will be as interesting to another person as what you get them to say about themselves**. "A person's toothache means more to that person than a famine in China which kills a million people.... Think of that the next time you start a conversation" (Carnegie 1936, p.51).

Kids don't like other kids who act "high and mighty." Adults don't either, actually. **No one is going to want to work with or hang out with someone who blurts out, shows off or doesn't really listen to others' ideas.** Really, would you? Where's the fun in that? **Everyone is happier when the entire group has an equal chance to contribute.** Stop that from happening, and the message you send is that you need to prove you are smarter, that you have better ideas and that you are just all-around more important than everyone else.

Take it from "Dictionary Brain." Control the urge to show off what you know (tips on that coming up), and contribute to the group little bits at a time. You don't have to have an encyclopedia full of facts ready, know just what to say or even have a bunch of funny jokes at your fingertips. The crazy, way-hidden, are-you-serious, very-secret social rule is this: **To learn a lot and be included more often, you have to become a really good listener.** Want to know how? Good. Keep listening.

9

Mirror! Mirror!

Reflect, Reflect, Reflect

Need-to-Knows

- You have to use your whole body to SHOW someone you are truly listening (remember: they can't tell you are paying attention unless you SHOW it).

- Reflective listening techniques help you stay focused and create strong connections with other people.

Asperkid Logic

By now, you've got the point that listening to people—not talking at them—is actually how to impress people and make them interested in knowing you better. Sounds pretty easy, right? Wrong. Being a good, active listener takes thought, preparation and lots and lots of practice. **It involves your body first and words last.** And while it sounds strange at first, it really is simple logic. By encouraging others to talk about themselves, you make people feel important. And when you make them feel important, they want to be around you more.

So, how do we get started?

Listening with Your Whole Body

Your ears may be all you need to hear, but you need a lot more to SHOW that you are listening. Remember, **the other person can't tell you are paying attention** unless you use your body to make it clear.

Eyes

This is tricky for Aspies. In general, NTs show interest by making and maintaining eye contact with the other person. For a lot of us, though, eye contact is really uncomfortable; we end up thinking more about trying to look at the person than what's being said.

Try:

- looking at the spot between the person's eyes, or at their nose; it will seem that you are looking at his eyes

- saying, "Forgive me—I'm really listening, sometimes I can pay attention better if I look away."

Mind

The human mind CANNOT think about two thoughts at the same time. It is a scientific fact. We can switch back and forth really fast, but we can't think about two things at once. This means that if you are thinking about what to say next, you are NOT listening to what the other person is saying. So if you are about to jump in with a "but..."—wait until you have heard her whole idea. You can't hear what she's saying if you are thinking about what your own reply will be.

Hands, feet, etc.

Bouncing around, squirming in your chair, fidgeting like crazy—these may not feel distracting to you. In fact, you may actually listen better if you have something to occupy your hands. But to the other person, it probably doesn't *feel* like you are listening. Moving around a whole lot sends the message that you are impatient or bored. So, you might say, "What you're saying is really important. I need to keep my hands busy or to move a bit so I can really listen well." And that should be absolutely fine.

Then, use the rest of your body to SHOW you're paying attention:

- Lean in, toward the speaker.
- Nod your head occasionally to show you understand.
- Smile, if it's a happy topic.
- Keep arms uncrossed; closing your body sends the message that you're not open to others' ideas.
- Ditch any gadgets, like cell phones or games. (Remember the point about not being able to think about two things at once? You really can't do it.)

Interrupting

Even though we don't mean it that way, **interrupting another person says that we don't really care about what he's saying and that what you have to say is more important**. This is a really common Aspie habit—and a tough one to break. So, how to stop?

- **Close your mouth.** Literally. If you have opened your mouth and are about to speak, shut it. Even without speaking, opening your mouth sends the message that you WANT to talk rather than listen. Imagine you have glue on your lips and keep them closed.

- **Imagine a notepad.** One of the main reasons we interrupt is because we are afraid we're going to forget what we want to say. So actually imagine a notepad, and "see" yourself writing your thought out. By visualizing the idea, you are a lot more likely to remember it. Or if you have a real notepad, use it.

Once your body is involved, your mind is more focused, too. Great start. You are well on your way to showing others that you hear them and that you are interested in what they say. Which means you are making others take more of an interest in you, and in what you will eventually say, too.

Mirror! Mirror!

You're leaning, nodding and listening. You've got that whole body thing working, making it clear to the person speaking that you are paying attention. She feels important. She feels interesting. And it's all because of you.

Which totally rocks. People act based on the thoughts and feelings they have about something or someone. By making the speaker feel important and interesting, you've given her really good thoughts about you.

You've got the rest of your body in the game—now let's bring that voice back.

Reflective Listening

After college, I went to graduate school to become a counselor (and then a teacher) for middle and high school kids. At that time, I still didn't know I was an Aspergirl—or even what Asperger's was. But I did know that one particular skill we were being taught made a big difference in the kinds of conversations I was able to have with people.

Without realizing it, I was learning to listen in a way that is totally un-Aspie...but is really, really powerful. It's a strategy called "reflective listening." And in my mind, I named it "being a mirror." Bear with me—at first it may sound a little "psycho-babble"—that stuff that counselors and psychologists use. Well, I did learn it in Social Work School, after all. But trust me, it works.

Reflective Listening lets other people know that not only are we listening, we are *understanding* them. For Aspies, understanding other people's ideas can be really tough. SHOWING that we understand is even harder—but to make others feel "heard," it's a "have to do."

This skill will make time spent with anyone—your parents, teachers, friends, guys/girls (as in dating), your future boss, even your brothers and sisters—easier and more sincere.

What It is…and What It isn't

Reflective Listening IS:

- a way to keep your mind from wandering while listening
- a way to make sure you understand what someone is *actually* saying and feeling, rather than what you *thought* they said or felt
- proof that you want to understand the speaker's ideas
- a way to help the speaker figure out his own thoughts, which makes him feel more powerful (and glad to be around you)
- the start of better, truer friendships.

Reflective Listening IS NOT:

- a way to prove you are right
- a method to persuade or convince someone to agree with you
- a statement on your part that you agree or disagree with the person's point of view, just that you understand it.

And here's how you do it:

Step 1: Reflect the Words

Say back (repeat or summarize) what you've heard, but in a question form beginning with:

"You feel..." or **"It sounds like you..."** or **"You're wondering if..."**

If you're reflecting the person correctly (being a good mirror), the speaker will say so.

If you're not quite getting the message (sort of like a fun-house mirror), the speaker should say that, too. It may even turn out that you did hear correctly, but that the person speaking isn't saying exactly what he means.

For example:

You hear a friend say: "I can't do anything right!"

You say: "You feel like you mess up a lot?"

Step 2: Reflect the Feeling

Challenge moment! Can you hear a particular feeling in the person's voice? That's tough, I know, but try. Is she speaking very quickly? Loudly? Quietly? Look at her body. Is she stomping her feet or are her shoulders slumping? Is she crying? Is she laughing? Is she blushing? These are all clues to the emotions that may be just under the surface. And, you may even help her realize what it is that she is actually feeling!

Good starters here are (fill in blanks with feeling words—see page 50):

"You feel (blank)?"

"You sound (blank)."

"You look (blank)."

"Are you feeling (blank)?"

For example:

> Your sister said: "That girl acts like such a princess."
>
> You could say: "You sound mad" or "You look sad" or "You seem upset."

Step 3: Check-In

Time to make sure you understand what the speaker is saying to you. Ask a question or two to be sure, using one of these lines:

"You feel (blank) about (blank). Is that right?"

"You feel (blank) when (blank)."

"You feel (blank) that (blank)."

And yes, it is OK to interrupt! Just start with, "Excuse me," and the other person won't feel cut-off. She will feel important.

For example:

> You heard your friend say: "My brother makes me feel so stupid."
>
> You could say: "You sound pretty frustrated about your brother. Is that right? Did something happen?"

Step 4: Believe

You don't have to solve the other person's problem; in fact, you shouldn't. Remember, we are trying to step OUT of that awful "know-it-all" or "bossy" role. **Often, people talk just because they trust you to listen, not because they want a solution. Your goal is to be that mirror—to reflect, not to judge or give advice.** So don't give your opinion unless asked. Instead… show that you believe in others' ability to solve problems.

Avoid

These responses actually get in the way of communicating. They shut down a conversation, and really don't help you listen:

"That was dumb."

"You're absolutely right."

"It's your fault."

"You're wrong."

"I think you're just (blank)."

"What you really need is..."

"This reminds me of the time when I..."

Instead, try

You want to *give* the speaker power and encourage problem-solving:

"So how are you going to handle that?"

"What do you think should happen?"

"What do you want to do next?"

"How do you feel about the whole thing?"

Empathy—that ability to anticipate and feel other people's emotions—is difficult for anyone to really nail. We all tend to advise, tell, agree or disagree from our own perspective. For Aspies, it's dang-near impossible. So don't be frustrated if this seems weird or fake, especially at first. It probably will feel that way to you, and may even sound a little bit that way to other people. So what? You're trying. And if you practice—with family, close friends, etc.—you will get good enough at it to become a much better listener. Which, to the rest of the world, makes you a whole lot more interesting to have around.

10

You're Welcome

The Power of Compliments

Need-to-Knows

- Compliments given to others aren't insults to you.
- Being able to give sincere compliments is the surest way to receive them.

- Specific compliments are the strongest.

- Graciously accept compliments with a simple smile and "thank you."

Asperkid Logic

I remember very clearly that my date had taken me roller skating that night. It was kind of a funny (and fun) thing to do, as I was nineteen and the average age of the kids around us was probably twelve. Anyway, we went inside where the spinning lights wound in circles and the music was cranked up. The clerk behind the counter, a very pretty girl close to my age, walked over to take our money.

"You have the prettiest eyeshadow," I said. And she did. The colors were soft and nicely blended—and as a girl, I knew full-well that this was not an easy skill to master. She looked at me for a minute, almost suspicious. Then, seeing my genuine grin, returned the smile. "Thank you very much," she said, obviously pleased. "I just bought these colors." "Well, they look great," I finished, and began to walk away with my date to put on our skates.

As we laced up, he looked at me, obviously impressed. "That was pretty amazing," he said. I hadn't the faintest clue what he meant. "You complimented her—and you meant it. You weren't just flattering her, you were saying something really nice." I shrugged and smiled, "No big deal. I was just being honest."

The big deal, I learned, is that women and girls rarely give one another genuine compliments. The thought seems to be that if I say something nice about you, either (1) I want something from you, or (2) I'm being false and catty. How ridiculous, I thought then. I still think that today.

Compliments should be like little gifts. Apparently, it's a lot more complicated than that, though. We Aspies—both guys and girls—add yet another layer. We tend to see a compliment given to someone else as a put-down to ourselves. It's that "me as the reference-point for the world" thing again. Psychologists call it "ego centrism (self-centered thoughts)." It's an Aspie Pitfall. And

I promise—it is a one-way ticket to sorrow and loneliness. As a favorite T-shirt I've seen says, "It really ISN'T all about me."

Compliments given to others are not insults to you in disguise.

If your teacher compliments another student's poetry, she doesn't mean yours is bad. This is not the time to say, "Oh, but come look at mine!" You'd create a competition where none existed, and look like a sore loser. Or if a coach said, "nice hustle" to someone else on the team, you wouldn't pipe up with a whiny, "I ran fast, too!" No one said you were a slowpoke.

Not being able to handle praise for someone else is our own insecurity talking. And it's not particularly attractive to be around. **We have to have room in our minds for other people to have talents and abilities without feeling threatened that we, suddenly, are worthless. Or at least worth less.**

Please know—as an Aspie myself—blending in isn't just hard for us, sometimes it can feel like the last thing on earth we'd want to do. Learning to be content as a member of a group, rather than always exceptional, is a risk. Will we even matter to anyone anymore?

The answer is yes, we do, and you will…more than ever. Look, every person has unique gifts to offer this world. That's not by accident. If every one of us were the best artist in class, who would sing on Broadway? If every scientist were the best chemist, who would study the stars? We Aspies often try to make ourselves stand out because we think blending in means disappearing. And that's terrifying! Wanting to feel important is probably one of the greatest forces in all the world. So, shy Aspies fade into the background, bolder Aspies seek attention and admiration to the extreme. But believe me, giving (or at least tolerating) praise to others does nothing to diminish your importance. In fact, it makes folks more likely to compliment you. Remember the Golden Rule? Do unto others…

The famous writer Ralph Waldo Emerson said that, "Every man I meet is in some way my superior. In that, I learn from him."

He didn't say, "I feel threatened by him." Or, I have to measure up to him. No, he said to sincerely look at what it is that every person can teach you. Look back—what was my date's reaction when I complimented another pretty girl? Did he suddenly look at my eyeshadow and think, "Her make-up isn't as nice?" Did he ditch me for the check-out girl? Hardly. He was impressed that I could appreciate someone else's gifts without feeling that my own were being challenged. **Your warm words about or to another person will not diminish you; just the opposite. You will shine with confidence and kindness.**

Compliments are like smiles—the more you give, the more you get.

How to Give a Good Compliment

Figuring out how to give a decent compliment seems pretty obvious. It's not, though. Flattery is easy—but not very sincere. And general compliments aren't too powerful.

Step 1: Be specific

"That dress looks really nice on you" is a lot stronger than "You look nice." "That was a really interesting question you asked in history today" is much better than "Good class today." The more specific you are about what you admire, the more you are showing that you are paying attention.

Step 2: Back it up

Give the "why?" to what you started. Why does that dress look nice? "That dress looks really nice on you *because* the color matches your eyes." Why was the question interesting? "That was a really interesting question you asked in history class *because* you brought up a point I'd never even considered."

Step 3: Keep it going

Compliments can be really great conversation starters. Just ask a question about the subject of the compliment to keep the talk going forward. For example, you've admired someone's Lego masterpiece. "Where did you find that set? I've never seen it before!" Or, in the case of the history question, "Have you read much about Churchill (or whatever the topic was)?"

You're Welcome

A sincere compliment is always a welcome lift to someone's day. Don't take away from that boost by challenging it, or being threatened by it. You have your own unique talents to offer, even if you're still in the process of discovering them (goodness knows, I am!). Give compliments—honestly and often. There will be people that reject them or even argue with you, but that's their problem, not yours. And when the compliments come your way (which they will), accept them graciously without fuss or fanfare. Smile, say "Thank you," and be proud of the praise you've earned.

Quotealicious

"*A person who is nice to you but is not nice to the waiter is not a nice person.*"

"People cry, not because they're weak, but because they have been strong for too long."

Giving a second chance is smart. But giving a third chance is ridiculous.

1 2 3

You do the best with what you have and you only get better from there.

11

Broken Spaghetti

The Benefits of Thinking Like a Wet Noodle

Need-to-Knows

- Leaders listen to others' ideas and respect them. Their minds are "flexible," like wet spaghetti.

- Being a rigid thinker ("my way is the only right way") is like being uncooked spaghetti. You break (or break down) when you're asked to change.

+ Change is the only thing that is certain.

+ If we can only handle the world as we expect it to be, we are going to snap, just like uncooked spaghetti.

Asperkid Logic

We already know that our Asper-thinking can be a little bit rigid. All or nothing. My way or the highway. Black or white. There's not a lot of room for "fuzzy" gray areas. You take this road, not another, to get where you need to go because it's the most efficient—no arguing. You buy pizza from one particular pizza joint because it's the best—no arguing. I'm going to be Batman, you be the Joker—because I said so. I'm being the teacher and you be the student; now do what I say. I'm not being bossy, I'm just right. After all, everyone's entitled to my opinion.

Yeah, I think you get the idea. It's a weird thing. We feel more comfortable being in charge so we can tell others how things really ought to go (with the best of intentions!), yet our managerial skills (that is, how well we encourage and lead others) are a bit of a weak point.

In almost every small group I can remember—high school Key Club (civics), my sorority, tennis, cheerleading, even my kids' preschool parent-teacher association!—I was vocal, logical and passionate. I knew a lot. And usually, at least at first, I was asked to be a leader. But then, kablooey. My less-than-fabulous people skills would show through and suddenly, I'd crash and burn. Apparently, being a good teacher (AKA "instructor" who shows everyone what to do and why) is very different from being a good leader (inspiring collaboration and enthusiastic teamwork).

It took me a while to figure out the disconnect, I have to admit. If I knew the most about something and was the most into it, shouldn't I also be in charge? Not for my own good, but for the good of…well, whatever the cause might be. Nope.

Aspie News Flash: Good leaders are not always the people who have collected the most facts or put in the most time; they don't waste time showing why they are right. **The best leaders**

can listen to others' ideas, respect and include them, and never ever say, "You're wrong."

In short, they are wet noodles. Wait. Doesn't being a wet noodle mean you're a wimp or pushover or something like that? Well, yes, in some cases, that's true. But for our purposes, it means a being flexible thinker. You'll see.

Aspies' thinking is, as I said, usually a tad rigid. We don't mean to be bossy, we're just sure that we are right. That is our most natural thinking style—and it has definite advantages. Shutting out the details and stress of endless options is calming— like shutting out bothersome "noise." It's easier, for example, to choose one position: for or against, yes or no. Answering either "A" or "B" is faster. It's more efficient. It's less tiring!

But it doesn't guarantee we'll find the best—or only—solution.

Rigid thinking is what I mean by "being uncooked spaghetti" (or uncooked noodles by any other name). Go to your kitchen and grab some—just look at it. Rigid, straight and narrow. Bend it too far out of shape and SNAP! It breaks. Bend us too far and SNAP! We break down.

The alternative is the wet noodle. It's stretchier, bendier, and all around more adaptable. **Flexible thinkers—the cooked spaghetti folks—are more able than we are to adapt to changes in routine, invent solutions to new problems, and change their goals as possibilities change.** In other words, no breakdowns. They twist and turn, but stay whole.

The Only Constant in the World

When you're young, everything feels like it takes forever. The line at the grocery store. Waiting for your driver's license. It's hard to see how fast everything changes. But it does change. Actually, **change is the only constant in life**. Friends move. We graduate and move to new schools. Pets pass away. No matter how hard we try to keep things the same, we can't. My dad died four years ago. Nothing I can do will bring him back. In college, every day I had dinner with the same bunch of girls at the same table at the same time. They were my "sisters," and still are precious to me. But now, I live hours away from them and haven't seen most of them in a decade. My kids—whom I love more than life—grow up a little more each day. There's a quote I saw, though, that makes it all OK. "Don't cry because it's over," some unknown person said. "Smile because it happened." Every change is just part of your still-unfolding life story.

The world is messy. It's unpredictable, and it is sometimes unfair. And that can be terrifying, I know. **No matter how many routines, calendars, visual schedules or plans we make, life will certainly be uncertain. And if we rigid thinkers can only handle understanding the world as we expect it, we are going to snap, too.** So there's one more change that has to happen: we have to become wet noodles. Or at least pasta al dente. Keep reading—cooking lessons ahead.

12

Boiling the Pasta

How to Make that Flexible Thinking Thing Happen

Need-to-Knows

- "Small group work" is a lifelong experience—it doesn't end after school does.

- How you say something is as important as what you say.

- Different doesn't mean wrong. There is usually more than one way to solve a problem well.

- Everyone feels that he or she is the most important, most interesting person in the world.

- Don't always say what *you* want to say or what *you* are feeling. Ask yourself what *the other person* might be feeling. And respond to *that*.

Asperkid Logic

Small group work was my least favorite thing to do in school. It always seemed that one member (or more) did almost nothing, while others toed the line. And then there was the whole problem of knowing what to do and how to do it—but not wanting to be called bossy or a know-it-all.

Couldn't I just please do this on my own?

Nope. Not then, and not later, either. I hate to tell you this, but small group work doesn't end when you graduate from middle school or high school. It's everywhere. It's almost always. Yes, you can choose sports—like martial arts—that let you operate on your own. Yes, you can choose a career—like being an author— where you get to think and work on your own a lot. But black- belts need to practice with sparring partners, and authors need to listen to their editors. University labs depend on research teams. Governments spend money and pass laws based on committee work. Juries decide whether a man goes free. Marriages are teams. So are families. Small group work is forever.

So, what do you do? How on earth can we Aspies collaborate more successfully? It all comes down to an old Aretha Franklin song: R-E-S-P-E-C-T.

Playing Well with Others

Showing respect for other people's opinions is not the same thing as agreeing with them. It just means that you accept their right to believe and be who and what they want to without your judgment. After all, we certainly don't like it when NTs judge us as being "weird" or "abnormal." We have to extend them the same courtesy. That's respect.

Being Uncooked Spaghetti: The Don'ts

If you're ready to try the flexible thinking thing, let's start with the stuff to avoid—and why:

+ **Never, ever tell someone that he is wrong** (that includes using other words that mean the same thing, like: "That's not right," or "Never…" or "How could you possibly think that…" etc.). He might be wrong and you may be right—but that's not the issue here. **Your goal isn't to be right— it's to work together efficiently and effectively.** If we say someone is wrong or dumb or otherwise insult a team member, we wound his pride. We embarrass him. Or frustrate him. Or both. And once we've hurt his feelings, no amount of logic or facts will win him over. Classmates don't want to work with us or pick us for teams. Teachers are irritated. Friends (or even people you may want to date) choose to hang out with other people.

+ Be careful. Without realizing it, you can send the message, "You're wrong," in other ways, too. **Your body and your voice have to show you are willing to at least respect other people's ideas.** That means no eye rolling, no annoyed sighs. No yelling or walking away. No quitting. Those are all ways of trashing people. Of sending the message, "You are such an idiot!" or "I am so much better than you are," or "I don't care about what you are saying." No matter how frustrated, angry, bored or annoyed you are, no matter how wrong you believe someone to be, that kind of reaction is completely and totally beneath us.

Being Uncooked Spaghetti: The Dos

+ Remember: the other person may be totally, completely and absolutely wrong in his facts, his reasoning, his approach, everything. But *he* doesn't think he's wrong. Which is why any time you put into pointing out his faults is wasted time. **To convince anyone of most anything, you have to**

figure out why he thinks and behaves as he does. You have to get inside his head—and that starts by listening.

- **Listen.** Reread "Mirror! Mirror!" (mini-chapter 9) to stay on top of those active and reflective listening skills, because the first "do" in any group or team is actually listening to the other people **without planning your own comeback**.

- **It's not what you say, it's how you say it.** That was always my mom's line to me. I think I maybe heard it a million times (seriously) growing up, but I suppose that's maybe because I needed to listen to her advice a little more. It's true. Gentle feedback is going to work a lot better than getting all aggressive. "I'd really like it if…" is a whole lot nicer than "Do it this way…" or "I think you should…"

- **Try responding to others' ideas with appreciation.** Remember in "So You Noticed a Kindness" (mini-chapter 3) we talked about how you can find something nice to say about any gift? Same strategy. We're not talking empty fluff, here—find and offer some honest recognition of another's contribution. "You did a lot of research!" or "That's a helpful idea," show appreciation and offer encouragement without agreeing with the conclusion.

- **Offer your idea as a question rather than as a demand or fact.** Use "and" instead of "but." It's a nicer conjunction. Try: "Have you also thought of…?" or "I was wondering if it might also work if we…?" or "OK. And also, what do you all think of…?"

- **Suggest reviewing the facts together.** One of the most famous "getting along with others" books ever written says, "Nobody will ever object to your saying, 'I may be wrong. Let's examine the facts'" (Carnegie 1936, p.67). So, you could say, "Do you agree?" or "Well, I actually had a different idea, but maybe I'm wrong. It wouldn't be the first time! Could we look at all the facts together?" Suddenly, you have built a team in which everyone has a voice.

That Whole Other Person's Point-of-View Thing Again

Henry Ford, inventor and automobile industry legend, said, "If there's any one secret of success, it lies in the ability to get the other person's point of view and see things from that person's angle as well as from your own." As a suspected Aspie himself, maybe it's not so surprising that Ford realized the value of perspective—it was probably as hard for him to figure out as it is for you and me.

I'll even take that a step further and say that not only is it important to hear each person's unique perspective, but to get at *why* they think that way. Personal experiences often have great impact on people's opinions. The family of a soldier may have a hard time tolerating anti-war discussions. Someone who's recently been dumped may not really want to hear why "love makes the world go 'round.'" The more you know about the person speaking, the better you understand why he believes what he does, what unique experiences he may be drawing upon, and what sensitive topics he may not wish to consider. In those cases, just steer clear. **When emotions are talking, logic is never going to prevail.**

The truth is that everyone wants to succeed. They want to feel smart and important and liked, just as you do. Trust that. I know it's hard to operate in a world where so much seems confusing. **One of the greatest fears we Aspies carry around with us all of the time is that we don't know what is coming.** We don't know what will happen or what someone will say or how they will react. So we pile on routine after schedule after appointment after ritual after rule to try to organize the world. And it doesn't work. We're still anxious.

So use this as a guideline: **Everyone feels that he or she is the most important, most interesting person in the world.** The next time you are in a conversation or paired up for a task, on a date or at a party—ask yourself, **"How would I feel if I were in her place? What would I want to hear?"** Don't respond with what *you* want to say or what *you* are feeling. Respond to what *she* might be feeling. With that one rule memorized, life won't ever feel as scary or as unpredictable, simply because you took the time to consider another's point of view. And you acted like a wet noodle.

13

You've Got to Hold the Pillow

Why Criticism Matters

Need-to-Knows

- No one enjoys criticism, but nothing improves without it.

- Black-and-white thinking (being uncooked spaghetti) can make it hard to really listen to a critique.

- "Old wounds" from bullying may make criticism feel like an actual attack, even if no one is actually out to hurt us.

- We have to be able to "hold the pillow" to learn and grow as people.

Asperkid Logic

When I submit a manuscript to my editors and publisher, I know what messages I want my words to get across to readers. I've thought about my audience and what I think you will want to know. I've considered my own experiences, and sorted through loads of memories, picking those that will most clearly illustrate my ideas. It's a lot of work—and more than that, there is a lot of heart tied up in these words. Putting it bluntly, I care what I put out there—and I care if you like it.

But before these words make it to you, they pass by copy-editors and publishing teams, marketing strategists and production departments. And that's scary. Every reader has an opinion. Which is why—no matter how good my original manuscript—I will receive "constructive criticism."

I'm going to ask you to try a little experiment. Pretend you have sat at a computer for hours (and hours, and hours) and poured your heart out to a world of strangers. When the feedback comes to your inbox, how will you react? OK. Hold that thought. We're coming back to it.

Criticism is scary. It is direct and intimidating. We all want to be liked (or loved) absolutely. And a critique can hurt. It can shake your confidence. But, let's be honest, it's the only way to find out what we can do better. And unless we are content being and doing everything for the rest of our lives as well as we can today, we have to learn to take it. More than that, we have to learn to use it.

No one likes being criticized, but Aspies have a particularly hard time managing it. Do you remember the "hold the pillow" demonstration I explained in the Introduction? Even if others' observations are soft and gentle (like a pillow), we Aspies often get more than a little freaked out when they are tossed our way. The point of that whole "pillow" deal is that if we dodge those pillows (which represent critiques) or we let them bounce off of us without taking hold of them, they are left lying around us, and they get tossed at us again and again. Probably harder each time. BUT…if we can catch the pillows—if we can calmly hold on to the feedback—there is quickly nothing left to throw at us. It's all over. And we are still standing.

I'm Right. You're Wrong. And That's That

For some of us, we are just too darned sure that our way is the right way; if our way of thinking is questioned or put down, it feels as though we, ourselves, are being disrespected. We're too invested.

When I was in college, I was the social chair for my sorority (kind of ironic for an Aspie, huh?). Among other things, I was in charge of our parties. During one particular semester, we'd been having a problem with members inviting more guests than they were allowed. This meant we'd run out of refreshments too fast, the lounge would get too crowded, and we'd have to spend more money on supplies than the budget could afford. I explained all of this at a general meeting. Everyone agreed that each girl should be allowed to give out two invitations only, which guests would then have to present for admission.

The evening of the next party, things were going smoothly— we were full but not over-crowded, the music was fun, everyone looked great and was having a blast. Then, there was a problem at the door. There were two senior guys who wanted to come in. They were nice guys, but were notorious for getting completely crazy…and they didn't have invitations. Politely (and nervously), I said they'd have to leave. However, our sorority president, a senior herself, stood at the door and told them to come on in anyway. Then she turned to me and said I was making a big deal out of nothing. "Quit being such a Goody-Two-Shoes," she told me. It was a party and everyone just wanted to have fun. And besides, I was just a lowly sophomore.

OK, I'm going to admit—I got mad. Really mad. And I said so. Even though I was two years her junior (meaning she outranked me in both officer position and age), she was breaking the rules. As far as I was concerned, I was running this party, and I was responsible for the budget. She had no right to tell me what to do and I said so.

Now let me paint that scene with fifteen extra years of perspective. We were actually both right. Which means we were actually both wrong, too.

As the leader of the organization and an upperclassman, the president should've pulled me aside privately and said politely that we were going to make an exception to the rule, rather than embarrassing me in public. Her style stunk. But you know what? She'd given enough of her time and talents to the group that she certainly deserved to have whomever she wanted at a party.

And, her criticism of me was true, too. I was so stuck on "the rule" that I was missing the larger picture—this was not something worth making a fuss over. Kicking the guys out would have upset them and probably a lot of their friends, who were already inside. I was being uncooked spaghetti, a rigid thinker. I was sure I was right and she was wrong. The bigger social consequences I might've caused never even crossed my mind.

Old Wounds

There is another reason Aspies can have a super-hard time handling a critical evaluation or disagreement. Many of us have already had enough criticism to last a lifetime. For those who have been bullied (by teachers, kids, even family members), more judgment just feels as if we're being attacked all over again. You can even listen to the word choices some of us use to describe the feedback: "I was… attacked, bashed, beat up." That's because the feeling is the same as if we've actually been thrown against a locker, cornered in a bathroom or scared on the playground. Again. We really do feel threatened. Or stupid. Less. Lonely. Rejected. Corrected or blamed. And that's just too much hurt to hold.

What do you do if someone is actually going to attack you? Fight or flight, right? You run or you hunker down and fight back with everything you have. My husband is really smart—the kind of guy who talks about quantum physics for fun. But school was awful for him. He has learning challenges, like attention deficit hyperactivity disorder (ADHD) and dyslexia, that were never diagnosed when he was a kid. So even though his IQ shows otherwise, he always felt dumb and got terrible grades. It's not too surprising, then, that any kind of criticism which makes him feel as though someone is questioning his intelligence gets him really riled up, really fast. That old instinct to protect himself is always close to the surface. He goes right to fight position—even balls up his fists or grits his teeth, and has to actually remind himself that no one in this house thinks or would say that he's "stupid." He's just hearing old "tapes" playing in his mind. And so, he can barely hear any value to the criticism above all the noise in his memory.

Editing

Truth. No one likes to be criticized. And to be fair, giving good feedback is really tough, too. But if a message is delivered well, by someone who cares, and if we can learn to "hold the pillow" (see the next rule!), really good changes take place. I promise.

It's been said that criticism is like a pain in your body, not particularly pleasant, but necessary. It calls your attention to fixing whatever is broken.

Remember my telling you about the editing process? The amazingly awesome thing that has happened is that I have learned whom I will trust and when to listen. I trust that I am a good writer. I trust that people who read books all day long want mine to matter, too. I trust my editors' insights, and they trust my passion. So now, I take a breath, open the email, and know that whatever words I read will help me create something better than I ever could have done on my own.

14

Take a Breath and Watch the Hammer

Knowing How to Handle Criticism

Need-to-Knows

- Criticism can bring you down. It can also build you up.
- Diffuse criticism from people you don't trust. Seek it out from people you do.
- The more defensively you react to criticism, the more likely it is true.
- Take a breath, "hold the pillow," listen and learn.

Asperkid Logic

"Constructive criticism" is a weird expression. It's sort of an oxymoron—like "jumbo shrimp." Criticism generally points out weaknesses, right? Not exactly a confidence-builder there.

True, no one likes to be told she's wrong. And it is really, really hard not to take criticism personally. There's that whole natural defensive reaction we talked about earlier. So, we shut our minds, dig our heels in—and either get stubborn, get mad, or get mean. Or maybe all three. And you know who loses? Nobody but us.

Imagine it this way: You see someone coming at you carrying a hammer—something powerful which can hurt you. So you cover your head or put up your fists, ready for the attack. Instead, though, stop a moment. Take a breath. That hammer is like criticism. **Criticism can be a tool for destruction, but also for construction.** It can knock you down or be just the tool you need to build yourself up.

Diffuse the Bomb, Value the Perspective

OK, you've been criticized. Do you think that the other person has more experience or information than you do? Your parent. An older brother. Your teacher. Do you trust that this person believes you can do or be better? If the answer is "No," and the person is just trying to get a reaction out of you, don't give it to him. When you get upset, you give up your power.

You've heard of diffusing a bomb? Well, you can diffuse mean-spirited criticism, too. If someone rants and raves at you about how dumb an idea is, or how your make-up is all wrong, **diffuse the criticism by indirectly AGREEING**.

It'd look like this: "You know (shake your head, or give a small laugh), that's a really interesting point. Thanks so much for bringing it up. I will be sure to give it the attention it deserves." [which, by the way, is none!] Now move or turn away. And congratulations! You have just told this person that her point wasn't even worth your time. It was ridiculous, and so was she. Well played, Asperkid. Well played.

When It *is* Someone You Trust

On the other hand, if the answer to "Do you trust this person?" is "yes," then the feedback is probably valuable. Take a breath, "hold the pillow," and listen.

We just spent a whole rule going over why criticism is particularly hard for Aspies to handle. So, even if we understand that it can be good for us, how do we accept it? In real life, you're going to be feeling strong emotions, so I'm not saying this is easy. Not even close. I'm just saying—from one Aspie to another—to get along in the NT world, this isn't optional. Being able to tolerate and use criticism is one of the main ways we are judged as being mature and together—or not.

Tip 1: It's Not about You

Constructive criticism is about an idea, action or thing. It's not actually about you. That's really important, so I'm going to say it again. **Constructive criticism is not about you.** It may be about *your* idea, *your* drawing, *your* performance, or *your* decision—but it's not a judgment of who you *are*, or of how smart or worthwhile you are as a person. **Do not mistake criticism of what you have done, created or said for a personal evaluation.**

Tip 2: The More Defensive You Get When You Hear It, the More Likely the Criticism is (At Least Partially) Right

Don't think so? OK, try this experiment. Let's say I walked over to you and said, "You are an old geezer." That's ridiculous, obviously. There's no truth to it at all. So you're not going to get upset.

What if I said something else, though. Something like, "You're weird." Well, it's not very nice, but you know what, we Aspies *are* a little different than most other people. We're *not* typical. So, there might be the tiniest bit of truth to that comment. You might even feel a little uncomfortable and get a little defensive. "What do you mean?" you may say. "Where do YOU get off calling ME weird?"

Now let's take the experiment to an extreme. What if I said, "You are a weird know-it-all and think you're better than everyone else. Nobody wants to be friends with you." THAT is going to get anyone going, but most especially an Aspie because it hits us in our most sensitive spot. We ARE afraid that no one wants to be our friend. And sometimes, it's even true.

Why am I telling you all of this? Because I think that last statement was the most awful thing anyone could say to you or any other Asperkid. And because I've had it said to me. I cried terribly—because I believed it was true. And it was, a little bit.

That's a danger for us Asperkids. We "break" these hidden rules, and end up sending all sorts of messages that we don't mean to. I didn't realize it, but a lot of times, I *did* sound like a know-it-all. And because of that, not too many people *did* want to be my friend. Oh, they had no business being mean—but I didn't make things better, either.

Think back to a time in your own life when somebody's comment really got to you. Now be honest—did it end up being true—even a little bit? Probably so, and that's why it bothered you.

Tip 3: Don't Wait for "Haters" to be Harsh or Cruel. Seek Out Criticism from Friends and People you Trust at a Pace You Can Take

If you are brave enough to listen, you may discover things you can change that will make your whole life better.

How? Even criticism from people you trust can be hard to swallow. But it's not impossible. Here's what you want to do to make the best use out of the advice they give:

1. **Wait for your body to calm down.** When you hear something that is difficult to absorb, your body is going to react. You may feel like you can't breathe or that your stomach has dropped to your shoes. You may feel hot or flushed. You may tense up. While this is happening, you're not able to listen or think clearly. Take slow, deep breaths. If you have to, imagine that the criticism is being directed at someone else. And most importantly, **DO NOT DO, SAY or WRITE ANYTHING UNTIL YOUR BODY IS CALM**.

2. **Close your mouth and open your mind.** Remember that you literally cannot listen to the feedback being given at the same time that you are thinking of what you want to say. Don't argue or defend yourself. Listen.

3. **Be confident. It's not about you.** Believe in yourself and your talents. Remind yourself that the criticism is NOT a personal attack. It's being given so that you can do and be the best you possible. Don't waste your time or energy defending anything—listen for the truth in the critique.

4. **Be a mirror.** Use those reflective listening skills. Restate the feedback that you hear. Be certain that you are receiving the message clearly. "So you feel/think (emotion/observation) about (your behavior/performance/idea) because (the criticism)." (Example: "So you feel concerned about the strength of my report because it doesn't include enough references?")

5. **Ask questions.** "What could I do differently? Do you have any suggestions? How would prefer I handle it? Did you know that…(fill in any missing facts)?" Be sure to get really specific directions for improvement. This is especially important if the critic is giving a general complaint without much of an explanation or suggestion attached. Asking questions will help you get the best advice and make the criticism as objective (about a thing, not about you) as possible.

6. **Say thank you and give it a try.** Once you're sure you understand the criticism and the suggested solution, thank the other person for his input and try out the advice. Let the feedback be a chance for you to make a change for the better.

We Aspies are really good at knowing every detail of what we believe and why we think it is correct. Hans Asperger himself said that Asperkids' parents should never be allowed to get into arguments with us because we could defend and argue our ideas without end. However, that doesn't mean we are always right or that we're the best we can be. There may, in fact, be other perspectives or facts we haven't considered. But the only way to discover them is for someone to tell us. So when you see a hammer in someone's hand—that is, you hear a criticism—remember to check: is he really there to bash you? Or is he there to offer exactly the tools you need to build a better you?

15

Speak in Sandwiches and Make Suggestions

Knowing How to Give Good Feedback

Need-to-Knows

- Avoid giving criticism if you can.
- If it is kind, true and necessary, you still have to package it well.
- Stay positive and specific, and always offer a solution.
- Critique ideas and actions rather than people.
- Sandwich everything between sincere compliments.

Asperkid Logic

You already know that one of the surest "hidden" rules is that people don't respond well to being told they are wrong. That's because frequently, criticism is meant to be hurtful, or it focuses on a person rather than on an idea, action or product. We've covered that, and it is all very true. But real life isn't Perfect World. We can't honestly say, "You are right about everything!" to everyone we meet. That's not being real.

For example: maybe you are redesigning your room, and your mom brings in a bunch of paint samples she thinks you will like; she's gone to a lot of trouble, but you think the colors are awful. You can't just smile while your bedroom turns sea-foam green. Or, what if your friend asks you to proofread his history paper, and it's not so great? If he's asking for your help, you owe him honest feedback.

So, here are two truths:

NT Truth #1: A lot of people ask for honesty when they don't want it.

NT Truth #2: A lot of people chicken out and don't give their honest opinions.

Have you ever watched the beginning rounds of talent shows like *Idol*? There are always contestants who audition truly believing that they are superstar material, even though they can't carry a tune in a bucket. Why? Because no one ever told them the truth. No one ever had the decency—or courage—to give honest feedback in a respectful, kind way. Most folks would rather tell a lie or say nothing at all. So, these poor contestants end up looking like fools on international television. That's just not fair.

When is it OK or necessary to give honest—but critical—feedback?

- to help someone achieve a goal or improve his performance
- to encourage a change (in a school rule, a favorite blog, a restaurant menu)
- to start or deepen a conversation (criticism of a book, movie, theory).

Criticism is not cool when it is meant:

- to insult someone
- to puff you up by putting others down
- to unleash complaints you've been storing up.

No one can escape that there are times when we *have* to—HAVE to—give critical feedback. And this is really hard to do well. But take comfort. Most NTs have a hard time gracefully giving criticism, too. So, be patient with yourself (and with others).

On my first day of work after college, my boss sat me down and said, "I don't mind if you have a complaint, but never bring it to me without a suggestion." **No matter how nicely you do manage to package a criticism, don't bother giving it if you don't have a solution to offer.** A suggestion should be useful, helpful—a clear route to improvement and change.

And STAY POSITIVE. A whole bunch of "Thou shall not's" is not particularly encouraging. That's why you want to steer clear of don'ts, and cant's and no's. Instead, use positive words—do, can, good, strong. So, you might say, "It would be great if," or "You can even," or "One thing that would make it even better…"

We've talked about the power of sincere compliments BUT if we constantly follow up our kind words with a judgment or correction, people start to distrust us. Instead of appreciating the compliment, they're waiting for the follow-up sucker punch. For instance, put yourself on the receiving end of this one:

> "You did well on that math test, honey, BUT next time I hope you'll do better on your English exam, too." Was that even a compliment? Ouch. Gee, thanks a lot for nothing.

How honest was the original compliment if it was really just "buttering you up" to knock you down later? **Instead of "but," if you need a connecting word, use "and."** It's a much more pleasant conjunction that doesn't prick at the ears or imply there's a bigger problem to come. Add in some praise for what's working, and just watch how the tone changes:

> "You did well on that math test, honey, AND as smart as you are and hard as you've been working, I'll bet you can bring all of your grades up that high. Your studying is really paying off!"

Last, **be clear and specific in your suggestions. Make sure you are focusing on actions, not on the person himself.** This will help the listener not to take the criticism personally, and instead be able to focus on actively improving. It might sound like: "The language in your opening paragraph is really strong. I'd love to hear more descriptions like that throughout the whole paper," or, "You looked so pretty in that green dress the other day. You should really keep wearing more bright colors like that!"

In particular, we Aspies have to watch our "mental filters" and decide how MUCH truth to tell…not to mention how it sounds on the receiving end. There is a famous question you might ask yourself before speaking, as well: "Is it true? Is it kind? Is it necessary?" (See mini-chapter 16, "Unfiltered," for more on this!) If you pass all three, move forward. And when you do have to say something that is less than "Yay!" say it in sandwiches.

Say It in Sandwiches

My family used to play a holiday game every Christmastime. Everyone would take turns swapping and stealing from a pile of mystery gifts. Adults and kids alike—everyone got in on the action. And, though her methods never changed from one year to the next, my "game show hostess" mom always managed to sucker someone. Without fail, the package with the loveliest wrapping paper, bows and glitter contained…a roll of toilet paper. Charmin Deluxe. That should've been a major disappointment, right? Especially after all of the stealing that was usually involved in snaring it. But the strange thing was that even if all of the other players wound up with fabulous trinkets, the toilet paper winner always had a big smile—because carefully and beautifully wrapped, almost anything seems like a prize.

Packaging is everything. And so, the first thing you have to remember when giving criticism is that you always want to begin and end with positive comments. You "sandwich" it, so to speak. If you start by saying something nice, the listener won't feel attacked. "Beginning with praise is like the dentist who begins his work with Novocaine. The patient still gets a drilling, but the Novocaine is pain-killing" (Carnegie 1936, p.108). By beginning your comments with honest, kind words, your audience won't get defensive and shut their ears before you have the chance to say anything more.

Along the same line, you want the last thing you say to also be complimentary. It sort of seals the experience for the listener, putting an "It's OK" memory stamp on your entire conversation.

Those two bits of praise are the slices of bread to your sandwich. Nestled between them is where you layer the actual critique, given in private, if at all possible.

By the way, you may have noticed that this book is full of examples of my own mistakes (I've got a load of them). However, I also happen to do a lot of things right. So why do I bother telling the entire world about the times when I've messed up? Because by pointing out my own blunders, it's a lot easier for you to face your own similar challenges without feeling embarrassed—you laugh and learn along with me, and don't feel so alone in considering your own areas for improvement. Use that strategy when giving criticism, too: **share your own mistakes before criticizing other people**. Pride goes before the fall. Let humility go before the criticism.

And there's your formula. Yes, it's still better to avoid giving criticism if possible. But when you do have to give fair and honest feedback, be sure to package it well:

Bread (sincere praise) + Criticism + Bread (sincere praise/encouragement)

Try to make sure the criticism:

- is given in private
- is sandwiched between sincere compliments
- begins with a mention of your own mistakes
- is positively stated
- is specific
- comes with a suggestion
- focuses on a thing or action, not a person
- is necessary.

When you've found yourself in an occasion where you have to give negative feedback, you can be honest AND helpful. Use our Sandwich Formula, and here are two examples of what you might get:

"Mom, it was so nice of you to get these paint samples for me, and I'd love it if you brought me with you to choose some others, too. Thanks. You really are a lot of help to me."

"William, your opening paragraph is really persuasive. And if you keep that message going as clearly on page two, then you will have a very strong essay."

Avoid giving criticism whenever possible, but if you must: "speak in sandwiches" and make specific suggestions. You know, it seems that once again, my mother was right (amazing how that keeps happening). It's not always what you say, it's how you say it that matters most.

Quotealicious

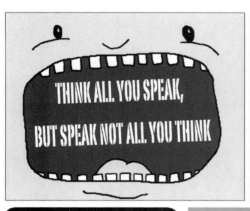

THINK ALL YOU SPEAK, BUT SPEAK NOT ALL YOU THINK

IT'S NOT WHO YOU ARE THAT HOLDS YOU BACK. IT'S WHO YOU THINK YOU ARE NOT.

Everyone has different strengths. We're supposed to. Otherwise it'd be like everyone adding flour to a bowl and expecting to get cookie dough. Someone has to be the chocolate chip.

Being brave means feeling afraid but doing it anyway.

16

Unfiltered

White Lies and Trust

Need-to-Knows

- NTs don't always mean what they say, especially when asking for "honest" opinions.
- NTs usually believe that lying is wrong UNLESS it is done to spare others' feelings or make a good impression.
- NTs tell "white" lies frequently—which is tough on Aspies, who take most everything at face value.
- Be sure to only trust those who have earned your confidence. You'll be taken advantage of otherwise.

Asperkid Logic

There seem to be three kinds of reactions when it comes to "talking about" people. There are those who will hear none of it. Think Thumper in *Bambi*. "If you can't say somethin' nice, don't say nothin' at all." Smart bunny. Then, there are folks who love hearing trash-talk. As one of my favorite characters in *Steel Magnolias* said, "If you can't say anything nice, come sit next to me." Those are dangerous people. Fun at a party—but you can bet that no secret is safe with them.

And then there are us. Aspies. We're the ones who end up saying something about others or to them that we don't mean to cause trouble. The "What did I say? I was just being honest!" moments.

There's that pesky other-person's-perspective thing again. Psychologists call it "theory of mind," but mostly, Aspies just ought to call it the Blind Spot. Because that really is what it's like isn't it? Figuring out what another person is thinking or feeling is so hard. Making life just that much tougher is the fact that NTs often don't actually mean what they say.

For example: just because someone asks for your honest opinion, she doesn't necessarily want it, especially if your opinion is negative. Or, if someone says he wants to know "all" about your collection, his version of "all" is probably not the same as yours. And if someone asks how you are doing, odds are she really doesn't want to know much more than "Great, thanks."

Bullet Points and White Lies

I've heard it said that Aspies are missing "mental filters," something to catch thoughts before they come out of our mouths and end up (accidentally) insulting or hurting people. I don't think that's the problem, though. If you want me to hold back or "sandwich" criticism, I can (heck, I just wrote a whole rule or two about how to do it!). We all can! It's just a hidden rule problem again.

Look, Aspies take things at face value. What you see is what you get. It's one of my favorite things about us. We say what we mean and we mean what we say. By our very natures, we value truth more than almost anything. And (here's the mistake) we assume other people do, too. So, we give information the way we want it—thoroughly and honestly. But often what the NT world really wants are bullet points and white lies.

"Little" white lies, fibs, half-truths. Little slips meant to protect yourself or someone else from being offended. A friend texts that he is on his way to meet you, but really is still at home getting dressed. It's an "unimportant" blurring of the lines. A little exaggeration, bending the story a bit. These are all "cute" NT world names for a not-so-cute thing. Lying.

Now, to most Aspies, a rule is a rule and a lie is a lie. We are all taught that lying is wrong; therefore, a "white" lie is also wrong. I realize that's a very "black or white" logic. But guess what, I'm an Aspie. That's me. So, I am not about to tell you that I think white lies are OK. I don't. Most NTs disagree, though. **The general "hidden" rule in NT world is that lying is wrong UNLESS it is done to spare others' feelings or make a good impression.** Which means you need to expect "white" lies to be a major part of daily conversations—much more frequently than you'd have to worry about noticing bold-faced, brazen lies. And that's really confusing for us, who tell and expect the truth. So, we get taken advantage of A LOT.

When I was in middle school (the worst of my years being bullied), I went to a sleepover party. At some point, a popular boy from our class called, and talked to a few of the girls. Then, they handed the phone to me. It was the boy's "cousin" on the line, they told me. He'd seen my picture and wanted to talk with me. This played out while the whole party egged me on (I was so nervous and so excited!)—he even called me at home the next week. Pretty soon, though, I found out that there was no cousin at all, just the boy himself changing his voice. The whole thing was just a giant prank between the girls at the party and the boy from our class to embarrass me. And it worked—because never in a million years would it have dawned on me that all of these people could be lying.

People in NT world lie a lot more frequently and easily than we do.

Why? They do it:

+ to avoid confrontation

+ to minimize problems (especially if they are responsible)

+ to exaggerate and seem more important

+ to gain power.

The best protection I can offer you from being "duped" like I was is this fair warning:

Acquaintances are not friends, and they have not earned your trust.

Trust can only be earned through time or authority.

Acquaintances are Not Friends

Most of the people you know are acquaintances. We're talking about someone you know—maybe even someone you see often. But this is not someone you know well, maybe the friend of a friend. An acquaintance isn't a friend, though a friendship may develop in the future. For now, you may see him or her at school or at a particular activity, but your relationship stays there—you don't spend free time together. Because you don't know him or her well, you can't trust that this person will not lie to you, remain friendly, or keep your confidences.

Trust Must be Earned

Only believe people once they have proven to be truthful and trustworthy over time (like a long-time friend) or by means of authority (a parent, teacher, the police).

At least as far as the receiving end goes, you've now been warned. Next, we'll get into the "too much truth" quicksand. Is there such a thing as being too honest? I don't think so—keep reading to see if you agree.

17

Tact and the Triple-Filter

How Honest is Too Honest?

Need-to-Knows

- Tact is knowing how, when, or whether to say what we are thinking.

- Being honest isn't the same as speaking every thought in your head.

- Before speaking, ask yourself: Is it true? Is it good or kind? Is it useful or necessary?

Asperkid Logic

First off, this is an opinion. Mine, and certainly not everyone's. I don't believe in lies—not big lies, not little lies, nothing. I want people to know that if I say something, you can count on the fact that it is true. However, HOW we tell the truth can make a BIG difference in the effect it has. We're talking about "tact," which is at least as important as honesty. Simply put: **tact means being honest in a way which spares others from having hurt feelings. It is knowing how, when or whether we ought to say what we are thinking.**

Think about it: if you told every person you met *every thought* you had about him or her, what would happen? People you like might feel unappreciated, unattractive, overweight, unintelligent, undervalued and unwanted. If people heard our every thought, we would lose their respect and damage relationships. In other words, **every thought doesn't have to be spoken aloud for us to remain honest**.

When I was a child, my grandmother took me on the New York City subway. In the car with us was a whole group of teenagers, completely working the "punk" thing. Tattoos. Mohawks. The whole bit. And I stared, open-mouthed. "Look!" I gasped aloud, pointing. My grandmother, worried I'd offend them, told me briskly to stop gaping—I might make someone angry. Actually, I thought they looked really cool. But her point was that staring and pointing is rude. And she was right. Drawing attention to people's differences may make them feel judged. Like they are "weird" or "less than" us, neither of which is a nice feeling to have.

Granted, I was a little kid, and kids say whatever they are thinking. But no one had asked for my thoughts on 1980s urban punk fashion. It wasn't a matter of being truthful. It was a matter of being tactful.

Enter the "Socrates Triple-Filter Test." A commonly told story goes that one afternoon in ancient Greece, Socrates (the famous philosopher) was visited by an acquaintance of his. Eager to share some juicy gossip, the man asked if Socrates would like to know the story he'd just heard about a friend of theirs. Socrates replied that before the man spoke, he needed to pass the "Triple-Filter" test.

The first filter, he explained, is Truth. "Have you made absolutely sure that what you are about to say is true?" The man shook his head. "No, I actually just heard about it, and..."

Socrates cut him off. "You don't know for certain that it is true, then. Is what you want to say something good or kind?" Again, the man shook his head. "No! Actually, just the opposite. You see..."

Socrates lifted his hand to stop the man speaking. "So you are not certain that what you want to say is true, and it isn't good or kind. One filter still remains, though, so you may yet still tell me. That is Usefulness or Necessity. Is this information useful or necessary to me?" A little defeated, the man slumped. "No, not really."

"Well, then," Socrates said, turning on his heel. "If what you want to say is neither true, nor good or kind, nor useful or necessary, please don't say anything at all."

Before you answer a question or voice your opinion, ask yourself: **Is it true? Is it good or kind? It is useful or necessary? If it passes those filters, speak up. If not, either find a tactful way to make it pass or keep it to yourself.**

Making Honesty Tactful

Many NTs presume that the truth will cause more trouble or harm than a simple "white lie." They mistake dishonesty for tact. They act as though they are in the position to decide what is best for the person being lied to—which sounds more than a little bit arrogant to me. When someone asks you a direct question, and brutal honesty may hurt or embarrass them, you can still be *tactfully* honest.

Imagine yourself on the receiving end of what you say before you say it. Focus any criticism on the product or idea, not on the person. For example, which of these replies would sit best with you?

Situation	Honest-but-Insensitive	Honest-and-Tactful
Your friend has a new pair of jeans, and asks if they are too tight.	"Yes! They make you look awful."	"Personally I always go a size up in skinny jeans—it's so hard to tell from one designer to another!"
Your friend's band has just released a new single. He wants to know what you think.	"You sounded like you were in pain!"	"I could tell you really put a lot of feeling into it."
The dinner at your grandmother's house is lousy, and she wants to know how you like it.	"Gram, this is just plain nasty."	"I can taste the love in every bite. Thanks for going to so much trouble for us."

Think It, Don't Speak It

Sometimes, being tactful has nothing to do with honesty—it just has to do with **keeping your mouth shut**. There are a few areas in particular where you might want to really watch what you say—or say nothing at all:

* **Money or material goods** (houses, cars, etc.)—how much or little a person (or her family) earns or has is none of anyone's business, nor should it matter. So don't ask about it or draw attention to it.

- **Religion/politics**—everyone has a different version of right. And usually, folks feel strongly about their beliefs. Be respectful of others' ideas even if you don't think they are so. Ask questions, if you want to learn more, and avoid calling one idea "right" or another "wrong."

- **Disabilities, physical or mental challenges**—they just don't matter. So, don't point them out.

- **Physical appearance**—positive or negative comments about someone's body shape, weight, skin color, height, etc. What someone looks like doesn't matter, anyway, so it's not worth mentioning.

- **"Behind closed doors"**—anything that happens behind a closed door (in a bathroom, bedroom, doctor's office, etc.) is meant to stay there. Talking about bodily functions and intimate dating relationships is not funny or cool.

- **"Out of sight"**—speaking about someone when he or she isn't there is unkind. It's also a bit cowardly. Keep your thoughts about someone either between you two or to yourself.

Extra note: Aspies are terrible liars. Hear me on this. **Don't try to say you've done something you haven't just because you think it sounds cool.** It doesn't, and you won't either. I promise.

Being honest doesn't mean being mean. Being real doesn't mean saying everything. So be careful. Give your opinion softly. If you don't, you probably won't be asked to give it again.

18

Literally?

What They Actually Mean

Need-to-Knows

- Aspies take things literally—but NTs don't speak literally. What they say and what they mean are not always the same thing.

- It's OK to get confused. We're not hard-wired to understand language the way NTs use it.

- Build yourself a team of trustworthy, patient NT "advisors." You can check in with them if you feel confused about a social situation.

Asperkid Logic

When I was getting ready to write this rule, I randomly thought of a friend of mine from college. After we graduated, she entered the foreign service and moved to Vietnam. Now this was a girl who'd been raised in the American Midwest. Working in an embassy in Vietnam was about as far out of her cultural comfort zone as I can imagine.

Anyway, in writing this rule, I recalled my girlfriend's job preparations. As foreign service workers train to assist ambassadors, they study the cultural practices of their host nations. Ten years later, those expectations are no longer in paper handbooks, they're all online. Curious to see what tips were offered to those coming to live in my own country, I went to my computer. And you know what? This stuff is Aspie GOLD! Cultural norms on everything from personal space to hand gestures. Just Google "travel etiquette to (your country)." You'll find out how to live where you already do—translated for those who don't speak the "native" cultural language (like us).

One of the sections I saw covered by many travel guides is "colloquialisms" or "vernacular," which basically just means common local phrases. And this is a really important "hidden" rule to learn, because Aspies understand language differently than NTs.

Let's start with what we know: Aspies take language literally. NTs don't. It's why idioms are so confusing for us ("sitting on top of the world" doesn't mean at the North Pole, etc.), why pronouns (I, you, me) get us all mixed up, and why we end up giving lengthy answers to people who really only want to say "Hi." Let me play "ambassador" and welcome you to a few of the MANY…

Situations Where What NTs Say and What They Mean are Not the Same Thing
Hello, Good-Bye and In-Between

- **"How are you?"**, **"What's up?"**, **"How's it going?"** and **"How are you doing?"** are meant to be pleasant greetings, not actual, genuine questions. Unless a medical doctor is asking, just say, "Great, thanks," or "Fine," or "Excellent." Follow up with "And how are you?"

- **"See you later"** and **"See you soon"** are also just polite expressions, and are often used even if the other person never expects (or wants) to see you again. Smile and say "See you!" in return.

- **"We really should get together"** or **"We have to stay in touch"** are the same kinds of generally friendly statements. Tricky point: in this case, the other person may, indeed, mean what he is saying. So, if he sets a time and date or asks to exchange email addresses or phone numbers, great. Otherwise, it was probably just a polite gesture. If you want to talk again, though, you can certainly ask how you could get in touch.

- **"Tell me all about it"** does not actually mean ALL about whatever the topic is. SUMMARIZE! What is the main idea you want to share? Let's say you're asked to tell a family friend about a new subject from school. "We're learning to identify the locations of European nations on political maps" is sufficient. If the other person wants to know more, he or she can ask.

Or, let's say you love Greek mythology (it's my daughter's special interest). **If someone asks to hear ALL about a subject, they really only want to know a couple of facts, maybe an interesting bit of trivia or simply why the topic interests you.** It's another "pleasantry," which is to say, polite expression that doesn't really mean what it says. We Aspies LOVE our special interests. But not everyone else feels the same. So keep your "all about it" answer short—maybe four or five sentences. You can always add, "And if you ever want to know more, just ask."

Handling Language Confusion

There are so many possibilities of say-one-thing-mean-another expressions, each different depending upon the country or region in which you live, the age of the person talking…trying to list every one wouldn't be nearly as worthwhile as giving you two strategies for knowing how to handle any language confusion.

Strategy 1: Be Aware of Yourself and How We Think

We Aspies are more likely to misunderstand other people. Between trying to watch body language, figure out sarcasm or tone of voice, and any other sensory distractions going on, it's sort of amazing how much we DO understand of the NT world. So, let's just accept it. We miss things. Main ideas. Connections. Things implied but never said outright.

Yes, we may miss something, but at least we are self-aware. We know who we are and how we operate. And when you do feel confused, that awareness can give you great comfort and power. Remind yourself that you're not confused because the world is chaotic or scary, or because you're dumb or clueless. You're confused because our particular hard-wiring sometimes gets in our way.

We're Aspies. And we have difficulty with non-literal language (people saying something other than what they mean). Be alert to the fact that, if you are feeling confused, trouble with non-literal language may well be the reason. Minds work in different ways, and knowing how yours operates is half the battle. **Being aware of our own challenges just reminds us to look harder for the connections and messages we miss.**

Strategy 2: Build a Team of Advisors

Every Aspie needs a small group (four maximum!) of NTs who we can trust to help us out. That can be parents, a therapist, peers, a sibling or a teacher. In fact, the more different perspectives you cover, the better.

For example, I have a few girlfriends who are my go-to's. In my mind, they are like a Team of Advisors. Each has her own area of particular knowledge, and each is a very different thinker than the others. One gal is extremely witty and creative. Another is exceedingly patient. A third is analytical and asks fantastic questions that really help me clarify my own ideas. And another is strong, warm and calming. Since I came to understand my "Aspie Blind Spots," it so much easier to ask them for help in understanding things I know I'm just not hard-wired to get. For example, if I get an email that I'm not sure how to interpret or have a social situation that throws me, I go to them.

And, by the way, there's no shame in asking for help. Everyone has his or her own battles to manage. One of my "advisors" happens to be hearing impaired; she's asked me to make phone calls for her because she can't do it. It's not her fault. She physically can't make the call and hear the speaker on the other end—I can, so I help her. And I can't always understand non-literal language— she can, so she helps me. There's really no difference.

Think of the folks you know and can trust. Choose patient, open-minded people who will take the time to learn about Aspie. And then, ask for help when you need it. Build your own Team of Advisors, and check in when you feel unsure of yourself. Once you are able to bounce your ideas off of someone else, you'll feel much more confident and in control.

Who knows, maybe you'll even teach your team to "speak a little bit of Aspie," while you're at it. (No, people, not literally.)

19

Do I Need an Umbrella or an Ark?

Sorting Mountains from Molehills

Need-to-Knows

- Aspies' black-and-white extreme-kind-of-thinking often leads us to believe problems are MUCH bigger than they actually are.

- We can go from Worry Level 1 to Worry Level 100 in a split second. This helps NOBODY, most especially ourselves.

- Stop panicking. Breathe. Look at the steps in your "Chain of Catastrophe"—and ask "Why might this *not* happen?"

- Empower yourself by imagining steps you can take to make things better.

Asperkid Logic

I picked my daughter up from school years ago, ready to bring her to gymnastics class. One week before, the girls had begun learning to do back walkovers—although for now, that just meant leaning backwards over a cushion bolster until her hands reached the ground. Teachers would help students then kick their feet over, and the girls would find themselves standing upright.

Here we were a week later in the car ride to practice. While she hadn't told me she was upset beforehand, I suddenly found my poor Asperkid in the middle of an absolute panic attack. She was crying, hyperventilating, flushed and barely understandable. Though she didn't even have her leotard on yet, and we weren't even half-way to the gym, she was already emotionally over the edge—frantic about the last ten minutes of class which MIGHT possibly involve more back rolls.

Even being upside-down was only a possibility, and even though one would never *make* her try it, she was a wreck. That kind of panic is called catastrophizing—it's sort of like calling the fire brigade to put out a major blaze when your sister's only burnt some popcorn.

Imagine this: I've asked you to stand up. Now, I'm going to send you on an errand (to the candy store—but you don't know that part yet). But suddenly—you've run away! Before I can tell you where I need you to go, what you might need to do there, or what you might need to bring along, you have already decided you're headed for trouble. You've gone out the door, down some street, around the corner and up a hill. You think that you know exactly where the "catastrophic" (horrible) situation is leading before even knowing what the actual facts are. That's catastrophizing.

I've done it myself, for sure. One autumn afternoon during my senior year in high school, I had to leave my last class, orchestra, early. My varsity tennis team had a match that was pretty far away, so the coach had given us permission to leave our last period a bit early. Well, I don't know if my music teacher simply didn't read the tennis coach's note or whether he had a chip on his shoulder, but the orchestra conductor flipped out at me.

He yelled in front of the entire class, and went so far as to write a letter to the principal saying that I had willfully disobeyed his orders. To be honest, when the administrator saw his note, she laughed—the idea that I'd be that bold or rude was just totally outlandish to her.

Still, we had to go through the drama of having a formal review. In the end, I was excused completely—but during the process, I was certain my entire future had been trashed. I'd already been accepted to an extremely prestigious university for the next year, and was up for a myriad of awards at graduation. Yet in my eyes, this one tiny misunderstanding was about to wipe away the fruits of seventeen years of hard work. The school would find out and reject me. I'd never have a good job or interesting career. I'd probably be boring…a failure…alone. My life—I was sure—was over.

Not so much. Everything was fine, and the only one who got in trouble was the teacher. But I was expecting the worst. It was a drop of rain, and I was busy building Noah's Ark II.

That's **catastrophic thinking**. Basically, it means mentally going from zero to Mach 100 in no seconds flat. **Your mind runs away with dire tragedies or utter failure, no matter how unlikely or ridiculous your logic.** It's imagining and getting completely stuck on the worst, most embarrassing, painful, devastating possible outcome of any little bump in the road. The kind of preoccupation that grabs a hold of your mind in the middle of the night and will not let go, mercilessly dragging you from one "what-if" to another.

NTs would call it "overreacting." Now I don't know about you, but I find that infuriating. If someone is mad or afraid, that feeling deserves respect. As Dr. Seuss (1954, p.47) said, "A person's a person, no matter how small." Or how Aspie. So I don't care how "dramatic" your feelings seem to someone else—you deserve not to be made fun of or dismissed.

Besides, **this isn't "over-reacting." It's Aspie-reacting.** Why? My opinion is that our either/or thinking and "my way's the only way" certainty can cause us some major grief. We don't see how any other (better) outcomes could possibly happen instead.

Take my situation, for example. I jumped from "My teacher wrote a referral" to "I will get kicked out of university before I begin and be forever humiliated," which on its own, is clearly a completely illogical crazy leap. But if you break it down flowchart style, it's not so implausible:

(1) Teacher Makes Referral to Principal → (2) Possible Disciplinary Action Added to Academic Record → (3) Final Records go to University → (4) Admissions Offer Withdrawn → (5) I Have to Explain to Everyone at School and Whole Family Why I May No Longer Attend the School → (6) I am a Public Failure and Object of Perpetual Ridicule. ARGH!

The secret to avoiding this craziness is stopping to realize that from one step to the next, our logic isn't always correct. Or even particularly reasonable. And always, always asking: "Why might this not happen?"

Let's use my own personal freakout to test the theory:

1. Teacher Referral: this happened. Ridiculous, but it was an actual event. So, we can't debate it.

2. Disciplinary Action: here's where the ACTUAL events didn't keep up with my imagination. Let's pretend we didn't know that yet. So, besides my fear of being punished… **"Why might this not happen?"** The administrator might listen to all of the facts, check with the teacher who wrote me the original excuse, and decide that the referral was unfair, dismissing it.

3. Final Records: **"Why might this not happen?"** If the administrator dismisses the referral, it never becomes a part of my records. And even if it did, one blip in an otherwise awesome record would seem strange—and probably not very reliable or important.

4. Admissions Withdrawal: **"Why might this not happen?"** The admission to the university was already offered and accepted. It would take a LOT more than a small misunderstanding or mistake to undo all of that.

By this point…the rest of the chain falls apart, because I've shown myself how very unlikely the other consequences are. Even better, I've taken the time to **remove the emotion from the equation and just examine the facts**. That gives us the chance to **take any action we might need to correct a mistake or prevent it from getting worse**.

And that's what I did. Before the meeting, I went to my tennis coach and asked her to write a note explaining that she'd excused me, and that I was right in following those directions. If the orchestra teacher had a problem with the excuse note, my coach pointed out, it should have been taken up with her—a peer—rather than taken out on me. I brought the explanation to the review meeting, and after listening politely to the orchestra teacher explain his point of view (not interrupting!), I presented my note and explained my perspective. I also apologized to the orchestra teacher if I had, in any way, been impolite (I hadn't been, but by showing respect, it made him feel better toward me and less embarrassed about his outburst).

Into every life a little rain must fall, said someone somewhere. That's true. When something goes wrong, it's as if there is cold rain falling on your face. You feel the dampening "wetness." But trust me—**every raindrop is not the beginning of a hurricane**. Evaluate the "Chain of Catastrophe" you're imagining to see how logical it is, and think about what you can do to make things better. It may turn out that all you need is an umbrella, not a rescue boat, after all.

20

Temper, Temper

There Will Be More Apple Juice Tomorrow

Need-to-Knows

- All conflicts have history. The time to act is before meltdowns occur.

- NTs don't understand that we melt down because we are feeling overwhelmed.

- We must clearly communicate and problem solve when we are calm. No one listens when we yell.

- Our bodies give us signals before a meltdown. Pay attention and choose to respond in a proactive way.

- Anticipate sensory overload and use your coping skills to relax and re-direct your energy.
- Tomorrow *is* another day.

Asperkid Logic

Forever ago, when I was a domestic violence counselor working for the police department, a strange report came across my desk. Like the stack of others on my desk, it was from an officer who'd been called to manage an argument that had gotten physical—but what made this particular report stand out was the officer's comment, written in marker. "What the ??" he'd written, with an arrow pointing to the following words, "the complainant stated that this argument took place over a tomato."

Really? I can see why the officer would've been upset. Here he is, voluntarily suiting up to go out there and put his life on the line, protecting those who need it from…tomatoes? What a colossal waste of time (and tax dollars), I'm sure he was thinking. And if the argument *had* really been about a tomato, he'd be absolutely right to feel so indignant. The thing is, though, that no one comes to blows over a vegetable (or fruit, if you're being picky).

Before the whole fight began, this couple was struggling with communication issues—who would spend whose money on what, when, who would be responsible for particular domestic tasks, and what fair expectations of one another might be. A tomato wasn't the issue. It was just a little, red representation of a much bigger problem between them.

Camels and Plate Tectonics

All conflicts have history. No war started "just because." And no camel's back broke under the first "straw."

Quarrels and strife don't spontaneously appear—they spring from actions taken one step too far or words inflicting one hurt too many. Your mom doesn't freak out because you've left toothpaste in the sink once. It's the hundred-and-seven times she's asked you to clean up before and the consistent disregard for her requests that makes her feel unimportant and upset. And you probably don't go ballistic because one person in one class gives you a hard time one day. Today's meltdown may be the product of years of relentless teasing by people who are nowhere in sight right now.

People are a lot like plate tectonics: before a volcanic eruption or an earthquake, there's a build-up of friction and stress. If we pay attention, there's a chance to escape the chaos. Yes, an explosion vents the energy—but it causes great damage and pain in the process.

The same is true between people and inside of a person. Before we "erupt," there's a build-up of tension—of misunderstandings, unrealistic expectations or (for Aspies) sensory input. And while that release of feelings might feel good in the short term, it does nothing but damage in the long run.

Which is why it's so important for all of us to practice our listening and communicating skills, and to say what we mean and mean what we say when tempers are calm, not when boiling points are breached.

We are Experiencing Technical Difficulties

The particular snag for Aspies, though, is that our emotional seismographs don't read very accurately. It's as if our little internal-stress-measuring equipment is experiencing technical difficulties. Because we struggle with interpreting body language, facial expressions, tone of voice and anticipating others' ideas, our perceptions of impending trouble can be off.

You might say we detect underground friction in Mexico, when the real eruption is about to occur in Japan. Or, we may not clearly communicate our own struggles with enough lead time for anyone to help. Our display gauge says everything's fine, when actually, there's a major internal combustion about to blow, and we're about to lose our cool.

When an Aspie melts down—cries, yells, runs and hides (and yes, I've done all of those)—it's because **we are overwhelmed with emotions that we don't have the words or tools to handle at that moment**. That's a legitimate problem. But, like the "tomato couple," to anyone watching, we just look ridiculous. NTs don't see (and may not care) about the frustration, panic or hurt that came first. They just see us freaking out. And it's not our best look.

I've heard it said that people cry not because they are weak, but because they've been strong for too long. Holding in your frustrations, hurt or fear doesn't make it go away—it just guarantees a bigger problem later...like stuffing all of your dirty laundry into a small closet. Eventually, you are going to open it and have the entire stinky pile fall on your head.

We have to face problems when we are calm, not when tempers are flaring. And throughout this book, we've already covered a lot of what you'll need to avoid those Dreaded Meltdowns: reflective listening, self-advocating, giving a good apology, and working with others. That's a start. But what about the solo meltdowns? How do we prevent those eruptions?

The trick is to:

- **Clearly communicate and problem solve while we are still calm (so others will want to help).**
- **Learn to listen to our bodies.**
- **Know how to calm ourselves down when we feel the temperature rising.**

It isn't a Temper Thing, But It Sure Looks That Way

Most of what the world sees as Aspie anger isn't anger—or temper, or rage. We usually melt down because we are feeling overwhelmed sensory-wise or have some expectations that aren't being met (regardless of whether they are realistic). Let's see what we can do about addressing those problems before they get too big to handle.

Sensory Stuff

This is a pretty easy fix if you take the time to anticipate what you can ahead of time. Make life a little smoother:

1. Choose shirts without tags.

2. Dress in layers: being able to cool down quickly will actually cool your emotions.

3. Earplugs can be pretty discreet, if you need them.

4. Keep a smooth "worry stone" or fidget in your pocket or desk.

5. Get permission to chew gum or suck on sour candies whenever you need them.

6. Arrange a "safe spot" with teachers, where you can go without stopping to ask for permission. It can be an outside swing, the nurse's office—I used a hidden corner of a dark, deserted hallway when I was in high school and needed to escape.

The goal is to shut out as much offensive sensory input as possible AND give your body whatever sensory input (often tactile or oral) it does need to bring it back down.

Expect the Unexpected

Oh, how we Aspies like our structure—our routines. The comfort of knowing what will happen on Tuesdays, where the cereal boxes should (or shouldn't) be placed, or how a shirt should or shouldn't be folded. It's how we try to control the great, big, crazy world of ours. Of course, it's completely pointless, too. The more rigid we get in how we think things need to be, the more upset we're going to be when (not if, but when) they turn out differently.

I've heard it said that the quickest way to make God laugh is to tell Him your plans. Now, whether you're an Orthodox Jew or a devout atheist, the point is the same. What upsets people the most is not what actually happens, but when what we expect to happen, doesn't. Now, if you stop to think about it, you know that the world doesn't run on your schedule any more than it runs on mine. You may not have your doctorate by the age you expect and your second child may not be a girl whom you name "Molly." In fact, as life moves on, you may decide to become a dentist and your children may all be boys. Plans change. Don't waste your energy or emotions protesting people or circumstances outside of your control.

Life doesn't actually *have* to work out the way you've imagined to be alright. You know that crazy-urgent feeling you get when suddenly, things seem to be going very wrong? That something has to change "right here, right now" or else disaster may ensue? You're being duped. Unless there's a fire, someone's hurt, or someone's about to be hurt, there is no actual emergency. The sense of urgency, of panic just means we've got that egocentrism thing happening again—we are seeing ourselves (and our wants/needs/ideas) as more important than others.

For example, my youngest son was in tears today—over apple juice. Well, not really over apple juice. You see, he drinks apple juice with breakfast every morning, but this morning, we'd run out. Now, even though I explained we'd have more by this afternoon, his expectations weren't met, his routine was busted, and he lost it. Thermal meltdown. An outsider looking in would've thought the house was on fire or he'd lost his favorite toy. But no. We were just out of apple juice. And although I had two other kids to get ready for school and a dog barking for her breakfast, he was going to let the world know about the injustice being done unto his little self.

What to Do, What to Do?

The reason young Aspies have more visible outbursts is that they don't have the words to express what they are feeling. When older Aspies haven't learned to "use our words" very well, we don't roll around on the floor, but we may lash out. We may snap at those we love, stomp off, slam doors, make snide remarks, hurt ourselves or just sink down into depression, heart disease or ulcers. Don't like the sound of those options? Good, because you have another choice. You can choose to suffer, or you can practice taking your (emotional) temperature, self-advocating, and self-soothing.

The first thing to do is to jot down things that might be bothering you while you are calm. Then, use your self-advocacy skills and your "I feel" statements to bring your concerns to someone who will listen. **If you only talk about problems when you are already upset, nothing will ever be solved.**

If trouble is brewing already, remember plate tectonics. Geologists know that every earthquake is preceded by "P-waves" or early shock waves. Those are the same seismic waves that animals often notice, allowing them to escape the turbulence to follow. Well, our bodies give "P-waves," too.

Take your emotional temperature:

+ Are your palms sweaty?
+ Is your face flushed?
+ Does your stomach feel sick?
+ Is your mind racing?
+ Is your chest tight?
+ Is your mouth dry?

These are your body's "P-waves" telling you that you must take action, an explosion is coming.

Remember my little Asperdude and the apple juice? Now, he's too young to be able to know what he needs when he gets upset, so it's up to me to teach him how to calm himself. As he gets older, though, I will expect my juice-lover to begin to weigh what really matters—to "reframe" the situation and try to see the bigger picture. I'll help him practice asking himself, "Is this small stuff or an actual big deal?" And eventually, he will be able to see that something like missing his favorite drink is disappointing, but not devastating.

But for today, my Asperkid's rant looked like a classic temper tantrum—a spoiled preschooler who needs to get over the "I want apple juice!" already. Now as Aspies, you and I know it's not that simple. Would yelling at him help? Or telling him to be quiet? No, that would be like pouring gasoline on a fire and expecting it to die down. **When we are upset, we need to know that other people hear our complaint, even if they can't or won't fix it.**

In the case of such a young guy, it was up to me to remain calm and say, "I'm really sorry you're so disappointed. I don't have apple, but I do have grape or orange. Which do you want, grape or orange?" He couldn't answer me right away, so I repeated his options, twice. When he still couldn't choose, I poured one glass of each and set them out for him (a safe distance away)—and in a few minutes, he sniffled, walked over and took the grape. The whole trouble was over.

But you're old enough that it's up to you to make yourself heard. And I promise you this:

A quiet, confident conversation echoes more powerfully than a loud, insecure tirade.

So, if you've recognized that you are getting upset, relax and re-direct.

- **Relax:** my kids learned from preschool to "smell the flowers and blow out the candles." It sounds silly, I know, but it's a proven fact that by altering your breathing patterns to become slower and deeper, you change the function of your body's autonomic nervous system. The "off" switch is flipped on your fight/flight instinct, and you buy yourself valuable control.

- **Re-direct rationally:** Aspies are great with logic, except when we're not in charge. The truth is that the world isn't fair, and it's most certainly not starring me or you. So give the issue at hand the importance it deserves—but no more than it deserves.

Let's review—because while this sounds like common sense, no-brainer stuff, when you are upset, it's very, very hard to do.

To Slam the Brakes on Meltdowns

- Talk about problems when everyone is calm. Listen to other people's ideas.

- Take your temperature and relax.

- If your "P-waves" are rising fast, **get away** until you are calmed. Say, "I need some space; I'll be back in (give a time frame)." Remember, though, **you DO have to come back**. That's part of the deal and of growing up.

- If you have some time before thermal meltdown occurs, take a few slow breaths and use those communication and listening skills to ask for help solving the problem. "I feel (blank) about (blank). I want (blank). How do you feel?"

- Get **past the impulse** to lash out or crumble. Remind yourself, "It's not all or nothing." Don't give away your power or dignity by losing your composure. Instead…

- Take charge. **Choose** to see your rising emotional thermometer as a signal to **USE COPING SKILLS NOW** (get space, take a nap, move your body, fidget, read a journal, take deep breaths, practice yoga, go for a run or walk, punch a punching bag, squish clay, read, draw/doodle/color, listen to music, etc.).

- When you are calmer, give the issue **the attention it deserves—no more and no less**. And remember, if you discover you did lose it, the mature, brave, humble thing to do is to take a step back and say, "You know what? I was being ridiculous. **Can we try that again?**"

You have every right to feel however you feel. I just don't want you to let the way you show those feelings get in the way of people listening to you. In the last scene of the classic book and movie, *Gone With the Wind*, Scarlett O'Hara—ever the procrastinator— is huddled on the floor as she wipes away her own tears. Her family is gone, her land and money lost, and her only love has just walked out on her. But (cue dramatic orchestral music) she looks to the camera, chin up and eyes glistening. She *can* muster one more ounce of strength, she *will* go on, defiantly proclaiming, "After all, tomorrow *is* another day!" Skip the hoop skirts and melodramatic tunes, but do take a lesson from Miss Scarlett. When you feel like you, too, have found your world to be quite lacking in comparison to what you expected, remember to reframe, relax and re-direct. Tomorrow *is* another day. And there will be more apple juice tomorrow.

Quotealicious

"Life isn't about waiting for the storm to pass, it's about learning to dance in the rain."

Sometimes, you have to take a step back and say, "Well, that was pretty ridiculous."

Look both ways.
(Perspectives. There are lots of 'em.)

Being an Aspie without a sense of humor is like being an accountant who stinks at math. It isn't gonna be pretty.

$$2 + \frac{2}{5}$$

21

The Science of a Greek Goddess

Hygeia, Aphrodite and Why They Were Such Good Pals

Need-to-Knows

- "Hygiene" comes from the name "Hygeia," the ancient Greek goddess of good health (best friend of the goddess of love and beauty).
- To be healthy, you have to be clean.

- NT world truth: people are going to judge you by how you present yourself.

- Being messy sends NTs the message that you are disorganized and irresponsible.

- Being clean makes you more pleasant to be around and more attractive to others.

- Personal grooming should happen and be discussed in private.

Asperkid Logic

If you sneeze in Spain, expect someone to say, "¡Salud!" or "Good health!" Instead of "Cheers!" in Italy, families raise their glasses and say, "Salut!" They are toasting health, life, well-being. In French, "sain" describes a healthy person and his lifestyle. All three words come down through the centuries from the name of a Roman goddess, Salus. In Greek, her name was Hygeia, the Greeks' goddess of good health (of the mind and body), and dearest friend of Aphrodite, goddess of love and beauty. So closely did she bind the ideas of wellness, health and cleanliness that her very name became our English word, "hygiene."

Hygiene means "good health" because of its namesake, the goddess Hygeia; it isn't a rating of how perfectly combed your hair is or isn't. What's with the history lesson? "Hygiene" is one of those words that makes teens squirm. That's especially true for Aspies, who may have had their "hygiene" questioned at one time or another. But the link between good health and being clean isn't new (Ancient Greece!), and this isn't some sneaky way of picking on Aspies. I'm NOT here to judge you or your individual fashion choices, either—I don't care if you prefer preppy, Goth, grunge, or if you could not possibly care less about brand-names. We're not talking fashion—we're talking health.

Any book of social rules would mention personal grooming habits. They're that important. For Aspies, though, the issue gets more complicated, thanks to sensory issues and that "theory of mind" (thinking about you thinking about me) stuff. Sensory-wise, washing, trimming and perfuming are not always easy. And perspective-wise, we're less likely to realize that how NTs see our hygiene affects our lives. So I'm going to tell you the truth about your body, and why it is no accident that Hygeia and Aphrodite were so buddy-buddy.

Trust me: this Hygeia rule is meant to guarantee you good physical and mental health. No taking anything personally, people. No one is criticizing you. It's just that I care about you. I want life to be the easiest for you that it possibly can be. I don't want you to be teased or bullied. And if I don't tell you this stuff, someone else will—but probably behind your back in a not-so-nice way.

Hygeia Says…

There's no debating this point: **being clean makes you and those around you healthier. It also makes you nicer to be around, which shows thought and respect for others.** This, I would point out, is why Hygeia and Aphrodite were probably such good friends. The goddess of love is not going to encourage folks to snuggle up to a smelly person.

You + Clean =

A You Who is Pleasant-to-be-Around and Much More Attractive

(Wink! Wink!)

Head to Toe(s): Let's Make It Happen

Alright. The personal grooming goal is to be an acceptably, healthy, non-smelly member of society. Here are some how-to's:

Where?

Grooming (brushing, trimming, clipping, shaving, washing, combing, flossing, putting on make-up) happens in a bathroom, or maybe at a bedroom mirror. Grooming should not ever take place in a public room (living room, kitchen, etc.) and most especially never near where people prepare or eat food.

With Whom?

Because it has to do with your body, grooming is a private issue. It is discussed with professionals (stylists, doctors) or people you know well (parents, close friends) in privacy, too, not in school or with others able to listen.

Clothes

Hygiene-wise, you need clean clothes—meaning fresh underwear and clothing that isn't stained, wrinkled or smelly.

Hair

It turns out the answer to how often you should shampoo your hair is a bit debatable. Some experts say daily, others say less so. In Western cultures, oily hair is thought to be the same as dirty hair, and a dirty scalp is like a fairground for bacteria. So you choose—**wash daily or every other day**. Use a dandruff shampoo if you need it. And if you have longish hair, use a conditioner after washing. Guys and girls should both comb or brush your hair thoroughly each day, and you may even want to try a styling product (like gel or mousse) to keep it under control. Last, **have your hair trimmed every 6–8 weeks maximum**, even if you're growing it out (more often if you're not). Well-cut hair is the healthiest hair.

Nails

Keep 'em washed, clipped (weekly), filed and clean, with cuticles trimmed. This goes for toes, too. You'll prevent hangnails, a nail fungus (like athlete's foot) and skin infections. Wash them after every bathroom visit. Girls—pedicures and manicures make this stuff easy; someone else does the work for you. And if you do use polish, keep it fresh or take it off.

Breath

Want to hear something nasty? Bad breath is caused by bacterial wastes which contain the same acids as you can find in decaying meat and sweaty feet. Ewwww. It's also really bad for your social life. So, brush your teeth AND tongue (the hangout for 90% of the bacteria in your mouth) twice a day. Use flossers if you don't like regular floss, and try an antibacterial mouth rinse. Chewing sugar free gum during the day helps, too.

Body Odor

When the bacteria that hang out in the warm, moist regions of your body break down fatty sweat, it stinks. Nice, huh? That's body odor, or BO. And if you don't think people notice it—you are very, very wrong. They will, and they will treat you as if you are dirty and gross. I've seen it happen to kids, and the worst part is that it is totally preventable. So, please:

- Shower daily.
- Use a combination antiperspirant/deodorant.
- Repeat the process after you've had a sweaty workout.
- Use moist towelettes in the restroom if you prefer—just be sure to get yourself thoroughly clean.
- Try using body powders containing corn starch; they absorb moisture, and can prevent odor and itching.

Perfume/cologne

A nice scent is lovely—but less is definitely more, and is never a replacement for antiperspirant/deodorant. You don't want to overwhelm other people or bother someone's allergies. Stick with light scents and use one or two spritzes maximum.

Shaving

Always, always, always use shaving lotion or cream and a sharp razor blade on warm, wet skin. If you don't, expect your skin to feel like it's on fire and develop lots of in-grown hairs. Shave in the direction the hair grows. Follow-up with a moisturizer every time.

Eyebrows

Keeping your facial skin clean includes tidying your brows (especially if you have any kind of monobrow happening). Trust me—it is more important than you realize. For first-timers, visit a salon or barber. They do this professionally, and will advise you on the best grooming method for you.

Skin

The most important things you do for your skin are to sleep well, drink lots of water, and wear sunscreen every day. Really. Besides that, you want to gently wash your face morning and evening with a face wash—NOT SOAP—meant for your skin type (they are in every drugstore for girls and guys). Gently rub your face with a washcloth to slough off dead skin cells (these are what get all clogged up with dirt and oil, and cause breakouts), and finish with an oil-free moisturizer. If you need it, use an acne cream, but never skip the moisturizer. Dry your skin out and it will produce MORE oil…and blemishes.

Make-Up

Ladies, you could have your make-up done in a department store or at a professional make-up counter the first time you're ready to buy. Ask for a clean, natural look and have the artist teach you what he/she is doing. You don't have to buy everything they are selling, but pay attention to the color choices, amount of product and method of application.

The Look

NT world truth: people are going to judge you by how you present yourself. And to most people, "clean" and "neat" mean the same thing. Think of it like a math equation:

If "clean" = "neat," then a neat appearance gives the impression of being clean, but a messy appearance gives the impression of being dirty.

That's why the NT world prefers "neat" to be part of your look. If you are trying to get a job and show up in wrinkled, frumpy clothes, I'd suggest you keep looking—you're not going to get that job. The truth may be that you have a lot things going on in your mind, and remembering to iron your khakis wasn't too high on the list. I hear that. Buy no-iron, wrinkle-free pants. In NT world (the world that admits you to schools and hires or fires you), **"unkempt" or "messy" personal grooming says, "I'm irresponsible, disorganized, and dirty, and I don't really care."**

Notice, please: I didn't say you *are* any of those things—I just said that they will *think* you are. And if you want a job, a date or a party invitation, what others *think* is true matters as much as what *is* true. The way in which you choose to present yourself to the world is sort of like your costume—your clothes, for example, didn't fall out of the sky onto your body. At some point, you chose them from a store and put them on. Maybe you thought the T-shirt was funny. We could say, then, that your shirt tells the world about your sense of humor. Or maybe you colored your hair blue to shock people into leaving you alone (rather a common defense mechanism, actually). Whatever you do, just know that you ARE making choices and creating an image, even if you don't think you are.

How Do I Do "Neat and Clean"?
Quick Wardrobe Tips for Guys and Girls

If you want to work the "hygeia" angle, but still want to look young and trendy, go to the mall and **COPY the outfits on the mannequins.** Ask a salesperson to help. Remember: big-wig designers made up the display outfits. Use their know-how and turn yourself into their model. Same goes for magazine ads. **Copy a look straight out of clothing catalogs, websites** (J.Crew, Abercrombie and Fitch, Hollister) **or teen fashion magazines** (*Teen Vogue*, *Marie Claire*). Order and wear with confidence— you're working a professionally put-together outfit!

Ask Them

I had to ask my mom to buy me my first stick of antiperspirant. I was embarrassed to ask, of course—and even though I wasn't smelly, I *was* the only one without a stick of "Secret" in my gym locker, so I felt babyish. A lot of times, adults don't realize that their son or daughter is really growing up. They may buy clothes that are a little too juvenile or overlook toiletry items you want to try. I'm hoping that the adults in your life will get you what you need without you having to bring it up. But if they don't, ask. I'm not saying this is easy—just that it's important. And from one Aspie to another, if I did it, you can, too. It will be worth your while. The goddesses said so.

22

Traveling by Bubble

Transparent Boundaries That Only NTs See

Need-to-Knows

- Aspies' mind-blindness keeps us from seeing boundaries between our ideas, feelings, bodies and possessions and other people's.

- Other people's feelings are as real to them as yours are to you.

- When we cross those invisible lines, we make NTs feel threatened, violated or offended.

- To protect themselves from further discomfort, they push "outsiders" away.

- Learning where NTs' boundaries are will help keep them comfortable around us and treating us well.

Asperkid Logic

Do you remember Glinda the Good Witch from *The Wizard of Oz*? She was the beloved, sparkly one floating above the Munchkins' heads. Not a bad ride. But we can't all travel by bubble. Aspies can't, anyway.

I've noticed, however, that NTs *do* travel in bubbles. Sort of. They live, think, speak, touch and interact with one another as though they each move in individual bubbles. To NTs, personal boundaries are as obvious as the shiny surface of an actual bubble. But Aspies don't see the edges of personal space. We just see the person.

Where we end and others begin is something of a mystery for us, though we don't stop to think much about it. Personally, I don't feel as though I walk in a transparent bubble, but in a transparent self. I can't imagine that there are ideas in my head or notions in my heart that everyone else can't already KNOW just by looking at me. It's like that Vulcan mind-meld thing from *Star Trek*. Touch me—heck see me—and everything I know is on display to you. I, like many other Aspies, hide nothing. We're like open books. We're the most loyal friends, not interested in two-timing anyone. We're transparent. Who you see is who we are; we can't keep up anything false or pretentious for long.

With Aspies, who you see is who you get. What we don't realize is—NTs are not like that. The person an NT presents to you is his or her own construction, bits and pieces of truth revealed strategically (and often bedazzled with an exaggeration or two) to create a public "image." And because we can't see the edges of our own ideas or the protective boundaries NTs build around themselves, we constantly "pop bubbles." We step over social lines, physically invade their space, blur private and public information and generally make NTs awfully uncomfortable.

It's Bigger than Space Invaders: It's Bubble Blindness!

It's a well-known fact that Aspies have a hard time with personal space. You've probably heard that from teachers, counselors, other kids. "Keep your hands to yourself!" or "Dude, back up." Speech and social skills counselors make a big priority of talking about "space invaders" and how you have to remember to leave an arm's-length of space between you and someone else. I've heard it suggested to imagine traveling around in a bubble (Glinda again!) as a way to visualize the cue. And yes. It's true—we do weird people out if we don't respect their personal space. I'm not dissing that point.

What I'm saying is there is a bigger picture. Our trouble isn't personal space issues. It isn't learning to communicate better. And it isn't giving too much information (TMI) or misjudging levels of friendship. Those are all just symptoms of bubble blindness! Our trouble is that we can't see borders between people or ideas. **We can't see clear edges where our "self" (our space, ideas, feelings, etc.) ends and another person's begins.**

Forgive yourself: until someone points out NTs' boundaries (and maybe even afterwards), we will invade personal space, personal information, personal belongings, and we will never mean a thing by it. I know you don't mean to be awkward or "weird." I don't either. Would you criticize a blind person because he couldn't see a car speeding past him? Of course not. So don't be upset with yourself for stepping over social lines you can't see. You CAN'T see them. You just have to know where to expect them.

Why? NTs don't realize you can't see what they see. They think we're being rude, flippant or disrespectful. And why wouldn't they? An NT who ignores social boundaries *is* being rude, flippant or disrespectful. We're just being Aspie.

You'd think that, as an author writing a book about this topic, I'd be darned good at avoiding the mind-blindness pitfalls myself. Sometimes I am. But not always. When I wrote out the book proposal of the very book you are reading, I included some of the examples of the rules I wanted to include. Thank goodness my publisher believes in my writing and had already published my first book, because I had a bit of a problem.

The proposal was written very clearly—if you could read my thoughts. Anyone else was in trouble. After all, what did I mean by rules like "Mirror! Mirror!" or "Boiling the Pasta"? You see, I hadn't explained what any of the rules would actually be about. Just because *I* knew what would be included under "Mirror! Mirror!" did not, of course, mean anyone else would. Apologetically, I sent a thorough explanation, adding, "I fear that more than a bit of my own mind-blindness may have interfered." And thank goodness, she listened.

Not everyone in every circumstance will listen, though. They aren't all so patient. That's why: **we must learn where NTs see social boundaries, and respect them as if we could see them, too**.

Where are the Bubbles' Edges?

Social boundaries are very real to NTs. And even if you can't see them, you know when you've crossed a line. It goes something like this:

- NTs see a protective space ("a bubble") around everyone's bodies, possessions, ideas and feelings.

- When we get too close to their bodies, possessions, ideas or feelings without permission, we "pop" the bubble.

- Or, if we expose our bodies, possessions, ideas, feelings or friendship without the NTs invitation, we "pop" the bubble.

- "Popped bubbles" leave the NT no protection. They feel threatened, violated or offended.

- To protect themselves, they move away or push us away.

It feels awful, right? As if we are somehow weird or repulsive. We don't need to be punished, though. What we really need is just a better explanation of:

NT "Bubble" Boundaries
Bodies
The distance you stand from another person is important, but complicated. How close is too close and how far is too far? Try this: imagine that everyone is walking around with a hula hoop around his midsection. If your hula hoop were to touch up against an NTs, you'd be at about the proper conversation distance to keep him or her feeling comfortable.

Closer together is the "intimate" zone, which NTs reserve only for family, pets, dating partners or very close (long-time) friends. Even with these people, it's good practice to ask before touching. For example, "Would you like a hug?" is always polite and a good way to check in.

Respecting body space includes not handling, displaying or discussing things which touch private parts of one's body, such as undergarments or personal hygiene items. Similarly, rooms where these items are kept (bedrooms and bathrooms) are meant to be off-limits to general visitors.

Last, **a busy body usually means a busy mind**. If someone's body is busy, don't interrupt with questions or requests. He will feel frazzled and may be short-tempered. Give him space now. Pick a quieter time and ask then.

Possessions
The rule here is one we've been taught as young children, yet without thinking, break frequently and carelessly:

Don't take things that aren't yours.

- Ask *before* touching, "borrowing" or using anyone else's ANYTHING—otherwise, it's called STEALING.
- Asking AS you reach for an item is not acceptable.
- Leave shared or public spaces (the kitchen, living room, bathroom, etc.) as you found them—without a trail of your belongings or trash cluttering "everyone's space."
- Leave drawers or doors closed unless they are yours.

- Return borrowed items before being asked for them.

- Treat others' things with even more care than you would your own.

- Show respect for other people's hard work, no matter how unimportant a job might seem to you.

Ideas

I had a boss who once told me that the most arrogant thing someone could do was to assume that he shared their opinion without ever asking him. He had a point. So, be on the safe side:

- Assume that any person with whom you speak has a completely different opinion than you do on politics, religion, and just about everything else until you find out otherwise.

- Everyone has the right to her own beliefs, no matter how ridiculous, strange or wrong you think those beliefs may be. Keep judgments to yourself.

- If you disagree with an opinion, you don't need to say so. That might start an argument. "That's an interesting way of looking at things" is a neutral reply that doesn't criticize or support what's been said.

- A different opinion isn't necessarily wrong.

- Ideas are intellectual property—using someone else's idea without clear permission is the same as stealing. It's also really tacky.

Feelings

Reality is awfully fuzzy. Some even say there is no reality—that perception is truth. I see a problem one way. That's my truth. My neighbor sees it another way. That's his truth. *Other people's feelings are as real to them as yours are to you.* Why does that matter? Because:

People react to *their* perceptions and feelings—not to *yours*.

Here's how it works:

- What you do and say creates feelings in others that you may not realize.
- No feeling is "stupid" or "ridiculous."
- Everyone has a right to his or her feelings. You do, too.
- Feelings cannot be wrong. Facts that lead to feelings *can* be wrong.
- Your feelings affect the thoughts you think, and the actions you take.
- Other people have other feelings, so they think different thoughts than you do, and will act differently, too.
- Positive feelings (relaxed, happy, proud, important) bring about positive reactions (kindness, including you, laughter).
- Negative feelings (embarrassed, hurt, afraid) bring about negative reactions (teasing, yelling, leaving you out).
- Having different feelings and thoughts doesn't mean one person is right and the other is wrong.
- We have to explain our impressions and feelings clearly. Other people cannot read our minds. They do not know what we are thinking or feeling unless we explain it. No matter how obvious you think your feelings are, communicate.
- We do not KNOW what someone else is thinking unless we ask.
- Use "I feel statements"—they can't be wrong. Say "I feel (emotion) about (behavior)."
- Check in! Say "Did you mean to make me feel (blank)?" or "Are you feeling (blank)?" Be sure you are reacting to facts not feelings.
- When people have feelings that you don't understand, it is good to ask *why* they feel as they do. For example, "So you feel (blank)? Can you help me understand why?"

If you want to influence others in any way (to like you, include you, give you a job, a date, whatever!), you *must* consider how you make them feel.

- Create positive feelings in others.
- Positive feelings create positive thoughts.
- Positive thoughts will lead to positive actions.

Bubblicious

There are a lot of people out there who claim to be mind-readers or telepaths. Personally, I think they are really just good information gatherers. Aspies are sort of "illiterate telepaths." We can't read minds. But we can gather information about what others may be feeling, thinking or doing. Do it enough, and you'll see patterns, too.

Imagining another person's point of view can be hard. Don't worry about what you don't know for sure. Try, instead, to build possibilities and maybes. Ask questions. Communicate your own ideas—remember, those are invisible, too. And all along, refer back to these "hidden" rules. Maybe you won't travel by bubble, but at least you won't get soap in your eyes.

23

Choices and Tactics

How to Recognize a Friend

Need-to-Knows

- The NT world has lots of "invisible" boundaries around friendships.
- You need to know exactly what a friend *is*, not just what a friend *isn't*.

- Carefully and purposefully choose the people in your life.

- Friendships aren't perfect because people aren't perfect. Even true friends make mistakes sometimes.

- A worthwhile friendship is one which makes you feel good about being you.

Asperkid Logic

Everyone says they know what a friend is. But do they? Do we? Dr. Tony Attwood, a psychologist, noticed that when asked what makes a good friend, Aspies usually answer with negatives (Attwood 2007). In other words, we say what a good friend *doesn't* do, rather than what he or she *does* do. Why? His guess is that we've had a whole lot of bad experiences with so-called "friends," so we know what they're *not* supposed to do. Unfortunately, we haven't had enough good experiences to give a solid idea of what friends *are* supposed to do. Makes sense to me.

It's awfully hard to describe something if you haven't really seen it before. Try describing my kitchen. Unless you've been here, you have no idea if it's big or small, cozy or modern, green, yellow or gray. And if you haven't had a good friend, it's not too easy to describe that either.

Friendship in books or on TV is tidy; problems are solved between the opening and closing theme songs. That's not the real world, though. In reality, friendship is murky. It's messy. And in NT world, there are actually a whole bunch of little layers between "friend" and "stranger." Miss those layers, and you will trust people you shouldn't. You may also scare away folks who could turn out to be wonderful friends.

So let's take a point from Dr. Attwood. In order to learn the NT world's friendship rules (and there are lots) we have to **define what a friend is, instead of what he or she isn't** (Attwood 2007).

A friend:

- calls or texts you about the same amount as you call or text him or her

- returns your calls
- writes Facebook posts on your wall and responds to yours
- keeps secrets
- shares secrets
- smiles when he or she sees you
- likes some of the same things you do
- likes some things that you don't
- shares some of the same opinions
- invites you to hang out
- waits for you
- introduces you to other friends
- saves you a seat
- stands up for you (even if you're not there)
- stops you if you put yourself down
- listens
- compliments you sincerely
- sees talents in you that you hadn't noticed
- knows your faults and accepts them
- tells you the truth
- says he or she is sorry and means it
- accepts your apology
- laughs with you, not at you
- doesn't pressure you to do things you don't want to
- tells an adult if you are in danger (yes, even secrets)
- will not always include you in everything he or she does
- means well, even when he or she makes a mistake
- likes you for exactly who you are.

That's quite a list. A tall order. Which is why it shouldn't surprise you to learn that in your entire lifetime, you may only make a handful or two of *good* friends. Count yourself lucky. It is the quality of your friends, not the quantity of them, that makes all the difference.

And even the best of friends mess up. That's one of the hardest things for Aspies to remember: people (like everything else) aren't all or nothing. Even among the closest friends, nobody likes everything about the other person. **No friendship is perfect because no person is perfect. Everyone has flaws. Everyone makes honest mistakes.**

Your choice to make is how willing are you to tolerate a particular flaw? One friend may be a bit of a grump. Another might be awfully forgetful. How important are those things when compared with their strengths? That's a personal call without a real right or wrong.

The Ingredients of a Trusted Friend

We can boil all of these particulars down to what you might call "the main ingredients" in cooking up a trusted friend:

- **It's a Two-Way Street:** friendships are based on respect for one another and an equal give-and-take of attention from both people.
- **Kindness:** friends like one another and try to make each other feel happy.
- **Perspective:** friends ask questions about each other's lives, feelings, and ideas, in order to understand each other's perspectives.
- **No One Loses:** true friends can disagree, argue, get mad, and solve problems together; staying friends is more important than proving who is right and wrong.
- **Things in Common:** friends aren't exactly alike, but they usually have a lot in common (interests, activities).

• **Slow Sharing:** over time, friends *very gradually* share ideas, wishes, and feelings that they don't tell others.

Above all, **a worthwhile friend makes you feel good about who you are.**

Pick 'Em

Why should you bother making friends, with all the effort it takes? I'm not going to lie to you—it is tough, and it does take effort. But do try. Life is better when you can choose *when* (not *if*) you'd like to be alone and *when* you'd like company.

Having the option to share your life with other people makes it richer. It makes happy days happier, and makes heartbreak easier to handle. Learning to see others' perspectives may spark ideas you'd never have had otherwise and inspire you to discover talents you never realized were yours.

Where and How?

Where do you look for friends? And how do you start? Start by remembering your goal: to discover *real* friends. The focus is quality, not quantity (one or two good friends are way better than a whole crowd of unreliable ones).

You already are exactly who you are supposed to be. Getting yourself nervous about what you should say and what you shouldn't do is going to make you try too hard. It'll come off weird and uncomfortable. Be you—don't fake an interest or say you know all about something you don't. Keep it real.

Remember, too, that less is often more. Bring the volume down and make your body quiet; although being loud or goofy can come with feeling nervous, it makes other people nervous, too.

Whom? AKA, Multiple Choice Mastery

The most important thing you can do (and the one where we Aspies have the worst track record) is **CHOOSING the right people to approach as possible friends. You want the right**

person—not just the obvious person. I've heard it said that we should imagine our decisions in our lives as if they are multiple choice tests. You probably already know that in an "a, b, c, or none of the above" scenario, one of those choices is always a "dummy" or trick answer—it looks right, but is actually very wrong. **It's a distraction.** Take it from me, a former teacher: find the "trick" answer FIRST, and get rid of it. It's a lot easier to see the better choice without the distraction. Know what? **Eliminating the "obvious" choice is a smart way to choosing good friends, too.**

For example, at school, kids in the center of the crowd may seem the most attractive. But they're pretty busy keeping themselves and the rest of the room entertained. **Eliminate the obvious choices—the people everyone else picked.**

Let's say your choices for possible friends are: (a) the girl with perfect hair and a legion of followers, (b) the shy boy who is a part-time magician, (c) the student council president or (d) none of the above. Most people will be faked out and go for (a) or (c). Those are the OBVIOUS answers, but not the best one. To them, one extra (easily replaced) friend probably isn't very important. You'd be disposable. The best choice is (b)! **Choose to approach kids who, like you, will be really value a friend and work hard to be good friends in return.**

Hi There

Alright. You've got a whole bunch of "secret" rules in your tool chest. Time to put what you know to good use. When you want to make a new friend:

- Smile.

- Try a little of everything—well-rounded people are interesting to be and to be around, so mix up your activities (music AND swimming or computer club AND an art class). This gets you around lots of different social circles.

- Notice—look at what someone is reading, wearing (T-shirt graphics), or doing for clues to their interests.

- Ask about their interests.

- Remember: have you spoken with this person before? What do you remember learning about what he likes or knows that you could bring up again?

- Talk to someone else who is on his own. Or, if there is a small group talking about a subject that interests you, walk over to the edge of the group and listen for a while before speaking.

- Read blogs and personal walls to see what people are up to.

- Give compliments.

- Take turns! Listen twice as much as you talk.

- Look for chances to talk about things other than the work if you are put in a small group or with a partner in school.

- Ask if your school or psychologist runs any social skills groups. These groups of kids (many Aspies!) create a low-pressure environment where you can practice hidden rules.

- Join a club or activity—try a new sport, or volunteer at a favorite charity. You may not think you are a "joiner," but there really is no better place to meet people. Whether your thing is drama, field hockey or Legos, there are clubs for everything. They're great ways to meet people with similar interests and give you instant conversation topics.

Whatever you decide to try, the most important tip is to get started. Don't get in the way of your own happiness. A journey of a thousand miles begins with a single step. A friendship of one hundred years begins with a simple "hello."

24

Who's Who, What's What

Friendship Levels and Cling Wrap

Need-to-Knows

- NTs see friendship in levels. Knowing them helps us to know who to trust and how much to trust them.

- It's better to be without a friend than to be mistreated by someone who says they are a friend.

- Keep friendships and conversations balanced; coming on too strong makes NTs uncomfortable.

- Friendships require more attention as they become more important.

Asperkid Logic

There's a campfire-kind of song a lot of kids learn called "Silver and Gold." You may know the words: "Make new friends, but keep the old. One is silver and the other gold." Partly, that's a message which is lost on you as a kid. After all, if your entire lifespan is ten or fifteen years, there is really no way to wrap your head around what might go into maintaining a friendship for twenty years. Last Christmas feels like ages ago! So, how old does a friendship have to be before it's "golden"?

It's not really a matter of time. The point of the song is another hidden NT truth: there are lots of levels of friendships. In middle school, I got "best friend" lockets with a girl I'd known less than a year. And I'm going to admit, I was thrilled! She was popular and I was really proud to walk around, the other "half" of the best friend team. We'd gotten very close over the summertime, and by the time school was in, we were BFFs. We had matching outfits, held sleepovers, told secrets, the whole bit. Yet within six months, another girl, who was jealous of the friendship, had convinced my friend that I was spreading rumors. She claimed I had been telling everyone I was smarter and richer and prettier (I'd said none of those things; heck, I couldn't even imagine doing those things!). And together, the two of them spent the rest of the school year plotting different ways to make me cry. I'm pretty sure that wasn't on the bullet points of what "A friend is…"

The truth is that I had no business having "best friend" lockets with her. Actually, the idea of having just one best friend is loaded with trouble. But that wasn't the problem. The problem was that we called the relationship something much more than it was—a few months is not an "old" or "golden" friendship. I never thought that someone who called herself a "friend" could be anything other than loyal and honest. I was a friend, and I was loyal and honest. I didn't gossip, and I never, ever meant to hurt anyone's feelings. My mom used to say that I thought that everyone would be the same kind of friend to me that I was to them. She was right. Being Aspie, it never occurred to me that other people didn't operate the same way…that they might use strategies, lies and drama, or that "friend" meant something totally different to them than it did to me. To us. To us, a smiling face is a trustworthy face. But that's not the truth for NTs.

In the NT world, there are many levels of friendship, and even though someone calls himself your friend, he may not be. Only time really tells who is a friend, and who isn't.

People aren't either/or. Relationships aren't either/or. NTs know this without being told. So they sort people into a lot more categories than we do. It keeps them safe. And you deserve to learn their operating systems, too. Just knowing they exist will help you figure out who to trust and how much to trust them.

Levels of Friends

An interesting way of looking at NTs' hidden friendship code is to imagine something called the Friendship Pyramid. It's the idea of the Social Thinking Clinic run by Michelle Garcia Winner and Dr. Pamela Crooke (see the Resources Section for some titles of theirs to try). Essentially, they describe a pyramid with five levels of people; my point to make to you is that people HAVE to pass THROUGH the bottom levels to get to the top, and that this *should* take more time than you think. Go slowly up the levels…

Friendly Greetings

Friendly greetings means the folks you pass as you come and go—it's most of the people you see like the school secretary, the check-out person at a store, kids you pass at the mall. Your goal with these people is to smile, if you feel comfortable, or maybe say hello and "How are you?"—basically politely just acknowledge that they are there. These are not people who expect you to speak more than a few lines of small talk. In general, I know a lot of Aspies see "small talk" or "chit chat" as meaningless or a nuisance, but it's REALLY not. Small talk is a chance to leave positive impressions of yourself on lots of people who, I promise you, are more important than you realize. For example, being friendly to a receptionist is not only just polite, it's smart: who do you think will help you get (or prevent you from getting) the appointment you want with that college admissions counselor? People you barely know may have great impact on your life.

Acquaintance

Acquaintances are people you don't plan to meet or hang out with, but whom you may see semi-regularly; they may be in a club or class with you. These are the people with whom you have short conversations (1–2 minutes), who it might be interesting to find out more about.

Possible Friendship

Possible friendships develop from acquaintances with whom you've had a few conversations, and then made plans together. So, maybe you and your lab partner decided to meet up at lunch period or after school. Or this is someone who "liked" you on Facebook or decided to follow your blog. This would be someone who it would be OK to walk up to, if he was standing with someone else, text about a homework question, ask to save you a seat on the bus. Your interactions are in public, and not very frequent.

Evolving Friendship

An evolving friendship is the level when a friendship demands more of your attention to keep going. Personally, I am not a big phone person—which is true of most Aspies I know. So, while yes, this would be a friend you could call and talk with after school or on the weekends, I'll also say that this is someone you could text or email/Facebook to see what they're up to or tell them about something funny that happened. You can also hang over at each other's house, go to a party together, meet at the movies. (This would also be the level that I would say would be OK to ask someone on a date.) Whether we're talking friends or dating, check to be sure they are reciprocating! Remember you want to keep the amount of contact and information sharing balanced. Check also that this is someone you want to choose as a friend. As you spend more time together, be sure he or she has all of the "ingredients" of making a good friend.

Bonded Friendship
Close to the level below it, bonded friendship means someone who has remained a friend over time—maybe a whole school year. You plan to hang out regularly and stay in touch consistently outside of school or practice. This is the friend you start to tell about feelings, crushes, fears…as long as you notice that she also shares her personal thoughts with you.

On Again, Off Again Friends
On again, off again friends may come and go between levels as interests change, but are people who you always enjoy no matter how close you remain.

Very Close Friend
Very close friends at the top of the pyramid are a really small group—really small—of friends you have known for a **long** time, and who have continued to be trustworthy, kind and sincere. This is a level that can only be earned with time.

Webs, Stop Signs and Cling Wrap
As you negotiate these friendship levels, there are some important things to know. The most important is to remember that you are a valuable person. No matter who says what, and no matter what happens, keep your head high.

When we forget to value ourselves, get lonely or believe bad things other people say, we get in trouble. We may get desperate or clingy, or come on too fast or too strong. We may share information that NTs think is too personal way too fast and hold on to friends too jealously. In the end, this kind of behavior makes NTs feel as if they've been hit by a tidal wave. They run. Or, they take advantage of us. It's why I cannot possibly tell you enough that:

Having just ANY person in your life is NOT better than having NO one.

I have put up with friends who wouldn't invite me to parties (they didn't want to admit we were friends) or would walk past me at school without acknowledging me. I was also in a physically dangerous relationship for almost two years in college because I thought I'd be happier having a popular boyfriend who hurt me or called me names than if I were single and safe.

- You are not someone to have to be endured.
- You are not lucky to just "get" whomever walks into your life.
- You get to choose the people you want: people who will treat you well.

Cling Wrap

There's an old rock song that says if you love something, you should set it free. If it comes back to you, it was meant to be. If it doesn't, it was never really yours to begin with. That's very true of people. It's understandable that if you've been lonely, you'll be excited at the prospect of having a new friend.

Caution Flag!

We've talked about "reciprocity" before—an even give-and-take between people. **Slow and steady wins the friend.** Take cues from the other person. Call, email, text, IM (instant message), stop by, or post at the same rate she does. Not more. **Listen more, talk less. That especially goes for your special interests.** It may be hard to imagine that others don't know or care about Star Wars,

Greek mythology, dog breeds, Tudor genealogy, dinosaurs, trains or whatever your particular passion might be—but it's probably true. And it doesn't make them dumb or boring. So, be careful. Remember, **you're looking for friends, not students**. And other kids don't want another teacher. Don't try to "convert" them or educate them about why they, too, should love what you do.

Check to be sure you ask about topics that interest others. **Conversations and games are give-and-take experiences, not one-person shows.** Are you having a two-player-dialogue, or are you starting to spew facts? Look at the other person's body language: is he or she looking elsewhere? Moving away? That's boredom! Stop where you are and say, "Sorry! Enough about me. What about you? What do you like to do for fun?" Use your listening skills to STAY on that topic rather than wandering back to your favorite. It may be tough, but the world is interesting because of all of the types of minds out there—other kids are still worth having as friends even if their interests differ.

Keep conversations, contact and effort balanced. Take everything slowly. If you are too afraid of being without someone, you will drive away the friends worth having. Being "clingy," overwhelming, coming on too strong. The surest way to ruin a new friendship is to overdo it.

Look for Stop Signs

Sometimes, for no particular reason, a friendship you'd like to begin just doesn't take. No blame. No big deal.

Ah, but there may be a translation problem. Some of the ways an NT shows a lack of interest in friendship (not returning calls/texts, avoiding eye contact) may seem unremarkable to you. We're famous for forgetting to return calls or getting caught up in what we're doing, and for not paying enough attention to our friends.

Be careful to recognize NTs' signs for what they are: a suggestion to step back before you make the other person uncomfortable. If a person turns his back on you, ignores you, or seems to be avoiding you, take the hint. Ease up. Quit the calls and posts, and don't be pushy. There are plenty of more friends to be made.

Take Care of What You Have

Ralph Waldo Emerson said that "the only way to have a friend is to be a friend." Friendships are like gardens—they need care and attention to survive.

If you have a friend who is reaching out to you and you don't do the same in return, your friendship is not going to last long. Friends need to feel that they are on your mind even if they aren't in front of your eyes. And while they may be in your thoughts, you have to SHOW it by keeping up your end of the relationship.

How? Little things go a long way. Remember birthdays. Cheer at sports events and concerts. Share funny links. Just be the kind of friend you'd like to have.

Different Friends for Different Things

No healthy friendship is an all or nothing thing. You know the expression about putting all of your eggs in one basket? That's too much pressure! No person can or should be everything to another person.

Instead, it's important for everyone to have more than one friend. So don't be scared or jealous if your friend has plans that don't involve you. Instead, take a lesson from the idea.

Imagine yourself as the center of a web or flower. Around you extend all of the different "kinds" of friends you have to fill all the different parts of your life. Start with one friend. Then add on. Maybe one person in your classroom loves gaming, while another kid in band is into the same movies you are. A girl from school wants to play tennis with you and a guy you know from chemistry wants to try building a robot together. You are not a one-dimensional person. There are LOTS of interesting, exciting things about you. And there are even more interesting, exciting people in the world! So start by making one friend. But don't stop. By having friends who enhance all different parts of your personality, you will become an all-around even more amazing person yourself.

WHAT WILL YOU DO TODAY THAT MAKES SOMEONE'S HEART SMILE?

You can't start the next chapter of your life if you keep re-reading the last one.

Let it go.

Here we are.
Together

BLOOM WHERE YOU ARE PLANTED.

25

Standing Up Straight

Self-Advocacy, Anger Band-Aids and Being Heard

Need-to-Knows

* Honestly knowing your strengths and needs is like having a superpower.

* Anger is a band-aid emotion. It's a real thing—but the wound you have to heal is underneath the anger.

* We teach others how they may treat us. We must respect ourselves before they will respect us.

* Self-advocacy means clearly expressing your rights in a calm way.

Asperkid Logic

You have a superpower. You may not realize it, but you do. No, I'm not talking about tights or capes or laser eyes (although they would be kind of awesome). You have something better—and a lot more real. You have the advantage of self-awareness.

"Know thyself, and you will possess the keys to the universe and the secrets of the gods" is an ancient, mystical proverb. It was spoken, some say, by the part-sorceress, part-prophetess Oracle of Delphi in ancient Greece. Most things spoken in ancient Greece have been lost to the ages, so what's the big deal about "know thyself"?

The Oracle spoke in riddles—like a fortune cookie. So, "know thyself" didn't mean that you must know your name, or know what you look like. She meant that you should be aware of your own wants, impulses, weaknesses, opinions, skills, strengths and passions. Great strength and great peace come from knowing who you are, and who you are not. You know that you are Aspie. I am, too. And that knowledge is our superpower. We know how we are likely to react in certain situations, yet (here's the power part) we can learn to CHOOSE our actions, instead of letting impulse take over.

This week, some people broke a promise to me. Bullies come in all shapes and ages. And this week, through no fault of my own, my trust was betrayed. I felt embarrassed, picked on and cheated. Well, maybe I still do. Here's the thing, though. I've been here before—when one person, for whatever reason (although it seems usually to be jealousy), has tried to steal my joy. There's an expression, "people throw rocks at shiny things." It's true. When you shine, you become a target.

The difference is I now have a superpower that I didn't have before. I know what I'm likely to do—I also know what I *want* to do instead.

When I learned of the recent trouble, a wise man (whom I call my Albus Dumbledore) pointed out that I was "shining." Other people were throwing rocks. I was good, I was right, and yes, I'd been wronged. Now I had a choice: would I be broken spaghetti, and rage? Would I send angry emails or yell or cry and make a scene? What would come of that? No power or justice—mostly just a loss of strength and of honor.

When we Aspies are angry, it's easy to give up or lose control. We may feel so hurt or so overpowered that we retreat in defeat. Or, we may lose our cool and become aggressive—calling names, screaming, protesting and whining. Then we just look foolish—our credibility and our power are gone.

Want to know a secret? **Anger is a band-aid feeling.** Like a plastic bandage, it is a protective layer—very real, but not what has to be healed to make you feel better. **Anger sits on top of loneliness, fear, shame or sorrow.** If we make a mess just dealing with our anger, we never get to fix the wound underneath. We're alone and we're still hurt—with some extra shame or loneliness piled on top.

You cannot change what you don't know (or won't admit) is true. That's why the Oracle was right: **KNOWING that you are likely to run or explode gives you the chance to stop and do neither. Instead, you have the chance to gracefully stand up for yourself—to self-advocate.**

Do not give up your power to those who would take it. As my Dumbledore reminded me, you must continue to shine—humbly—but shine, nonetheless. Quoting an ancient Chinese poet, Lao Tzu, he told me:

Achieve results,
But never glory in them.
Achieve results,
But never boast.
Achieve results,
But never be proud.
Achieve results,
Because this is the natural way.
Achieve results,
But not through violence.

(Henricks 1989, p.82)

Instead of losing control or losing my dignity, I literally stopped, breathed and waited. And it made every bit of difference—I took my time, gathered my facts, and stayed calm.

The NT world rewards careful action. What you do (or don't do) matters much more than what you say. By keeping cool, I was able to think about what I really wanted. I took a risk, and stood up for myself. Yes, of course I was totally scared the whole time—but being brave means feeling scared but doing it anyway. So I was brave. I decided that I was worth standing up for, and so are you.

Motivated by a great love (for Asperkids!), I made a clear list of unarguable facts, not opinions or feelings. I asked for, and received, an apology. And, by taking the time to really listen to some other ideas, was able to suggest "middle-ground" solutions. In the end, I won. No, the situation didn't get solved as I'd have liked. But that wasn't what I was really after—that's beyond my control. My goal was to act in a way that would make myself proud. And for maybe the first time I can ever remember, I am very, very proud.

When you are upset, you CAN stay strong AND flexible if you:

• Stop. Don't react immediately. Don't speak.

• Breathe. Several times, slowly. This calms your nervous system and gets you out of the fight/flight mode.

- Squeeze—squeeze a stress ball, push your palms together. This calms your body and gives you someplace to send your energy.

- Get some privacy if you can and WAIT (it will be hard, I know, but it's worth it). Wait until you can check in with someone you trust or at least until you have had time to calm down.

- React with facts not with feeling. This is one of the weirdest switcheroos. When we're upset, we lose our Aspie logic and get too emotional. **The NT world will respect you for clearly, calmly presenting facts; they won't change a thing just to suit your feelings.**

Put together, it's called **self-advocacy**. It's what I finally did for myself, and what you can do, too.

Teaching the World How to Treat You

I've heard it said that we teach other people how to treat us. I think that's very true. **Self-advocacy is teaching other people to treat us with dignity and respect. It is asking for what we deserve, and not accepting anything less.**

If you tolerate poor treatment, you teach people to treat you poorly. If you politely and calmly demand what your deserve, you teach them that you expect respect, fairness and honesty. It's your choice. **If you won't respect yourself, why should anyone else?**

Self-advocacy happens in a series of steps:

1. Know Your Strengths, Know Your Needs

As Aspies, we have some strengths in common. For example, as a group we have great:

- passion for our interests
- compassion
- honesty

- integrity
- loyalty
- logical and analytical thinking
- mechanical abilities
- creative abilities.

We also have some qualities that present specific needs:

We have this quality...	So we often have these needs...
intense focus on a special interest	reminders to ask about others' interests and not do all the talking
sincere, trusting and loyal	group of trusted NTs who will help us see others' (less honest) motivations
impulsiveness	strategies to calm ourselves and help us wait before acting or speaking
all-or-nothing thinking	problem-solving techniques, help including others' ideas
anxiety	coping techniques (like exercise, role-playing social situations, or just knowing who/how to ask for help)

2. Identify Your Goals

You are the main character in your own life story. You are the only one who can set the goals and make them happen. If you want something badly enough, you will find a way. If not, you will find an excuse.

While you might think that your goal is to punch a bully in the face or to somehow get revenge on the mean girls, that's not true. Well, not *really*.

Every day in every situation, you will feel better if you:

- stay true to your values
- say what you mean and mean what you say

- learn something new

- are brave and move forward, even when you are afraid

- remember that you cannot be conquered unless you allow it.

So don't allow it.

Stay focused. What do you *really* want out of this moment?

Choose one or two SPECIFIC, MEASURABLE goals that are within your control. For example: I want to ask that girl to have coffee. (The goal is *asking*, not getting a "yes." You can't control that.) Or, I want to audition for a play, even though I've never acted before. (The goal is having the guts to *try out*, not to get a part. That's someone else's choice.)

Ask for advice. Choose someone you really admire to be a mentor who will help you make your goals crystal-clear.

Then, stay calm. And keep breathing.

3. Know Your Rights, Accept Your Responsibilities
Your rights and responsibilities change from situation to situation.

School
Ask teachers for a grading rubric. This is a visual organizer which explains exactly what is expected of you in order to earn a particular mark (A, B, C, etc.). It's a way of being sure you know what's expected of you AND guaranteeing that you get the grade you deserve when you do the work asked of you. As an adult, this is the same type of document that would be considered a legal contract or a job evaluation (your pay depends on those!).

Everywhere
You have the right to expect that other people will:

- be honest with you

- keep their promises

- speak politely to you

- touch you in kind ways, and only if you say it is OK
- apologize when they have done wrong
- speak only truth about you.

However, you should also expect that they **won't** always do as they should.

That's when it's up to you to communicate—to teach them how to treat you.

4. Communicate to Others

Explain your ideas using three-part "I" statements:

1. "I feel or felt (blank) when you (describe the behavior)."

2. What is the effect on you? Tell how the behavior affects you specifically.

3. "I'd prefer or like (what you want)."

An example would be: "I felt really frustrated when you didn't buy the supplies for our project like you said you would. I can't turn in my part of the project on time without those supplies. I'd like for you to come with me and explain the situation to the teacher tomorrow."

You may wish to present your ideas in writing. This gives you the chance to think about your particular goals, choose your words carefully, and to be really certain of what you want to say. Read and then reread your writing. Reread it again. Walk away and take a break. Then come back and read it later.

Go to your mentor; check that your words send the same message you have in mind. Be aware that reality isn't, well, fixed or nailed down. Each person knows and experiences the world through his or her perceptions. Asking your trusted NT (a teacher, a counselor, a parent or friend) to hear or read your ideas is the best way to be sure that your message says what you want it to say.

When you are sure you have all of your facts correct, reach out with kindness and an open mind. Use those active listening skills! Be a wet noodle, open to reasonable compromises.

Stand Up Straight

Fellow Aspies, this is the only life you get. And you're in charge of it. The hidden rule is that **the world will treat you as you allow**.

Eleanor Roosevelt famously said, "No one can make you feel inferior without your consent." So what will you ask of the world? And HOW will you ask it? Will you be bossy, whiny or angry? Will you give up or give in?

Or will you be confidently, calmly assertive? Heaven knows if I did it, you can, too. Stop. Breathe. Think. Then go out there and make yourself proud of you.

Shine. And don't let anyone ever stop you.

Talking to Myself

Inner Dialogues and Old Tapes

Need-to-Knows

* Judging your own value by how many people "like" you is a recipe for failure.

* You must be the first to respect yourself.

* Having dignity means that you will NOT cooperate with anything or anyone that humiliates you.

* If you believe you are worthy and strong, you will live up to that truth. If you believe you are unworthy of love or happiness, you will live up to that truth, too.

* NTs say confidence and dignity are the most attractive qualities someone can have.

Asperkid Logic

WOO. Two years ago, I took a personality inventory that was supposed to determine my five greatest natural strengths. Other people were apparently "energizers" and "leaders." My results said, "WOO." WOO? What the heck was that supposed to mean?!

"WOO," apparently, stands for "Winning Other People Over," and describes people who enjoy the challenge of meeting people and winning new friends. Instead of being afraid of or put off by strangers, we "WOOs" are attracted to the process of collecting names, discovering common interests and—better yet—common acquaintances. Doesn't sound very Aspie, does it? It can be, though.

"WOOs," you see, are perfectly happy making a connection and then wrapping it up and moving on to new crowds, new people, and (I would add) new information. It's not about creating deep friendships but about collecting acquaintances. Understanding people and the patterns that link them, I think, became a bit of my own special interest. In a way, the more I understood of what they did and why they did it, the better I could protect myself BEFORE someone hurt me.

It turned out that I was a WOO after all. It was my defense strategy. My goal often was—often is?—win as many people over to "liking" me as possible. They didn't have to be my BFFs, as long as they weren't my enemies, I would be happy.

Except for that is a crazy way to live. You may remember that **personal goals have to be things that we can control**, otherwise how can we take credit for whether we succeed or fail? If my goal is for a thunderstorm to roll through my street tomorrow night—am I really to blame if it doesn't? Am I really to be congratulated if it does? Of course not! I can't control the weather any more than I can control whether people like me. Yes, I can try to be the most pleasant, respectful person I can be, but beyond that, it's not up to me.

Who Loves You?

Judging your own value by how many people "like" you is a recipe for failure. No matter what you do, no matter how wonderful you are, not all of them will. **The quality of friends matters, not the quantity of them.** When we, as Aspies, put our own self-worth up for sale in a world that doesn't even really "get" our basic operating system, we set ourselves up to fail.

Grown-ups tell little children that everyone should be friends with everyone else. That's not the way it really works, though. Everyone is "supposed" to love each other. But they don't. **Not everyone is going to love me—or you.** Sometimes, it's other kids who give you grief, sometimes it's an adult—I remember even having a teacher pick on me. Now, if that kind of thing truly doesn't bother you, then consider yourself truly and hugely blessed.

If, however, you are a little more "WOO-ish," and spend your energy trying to make everyone like you or (even sadder) to change yourself (your hair, your clothes, your voice, your body, your brains) into what you THINK they'll like…stop. Now. You're going to get really tired. You're going to be used, tricked, and let down. You will feel hollow. And worst of all, you won't even have the best friend you are supposed to have—yourself. As Judy Garland said, "Always be a first-rate version of yourself, instead of a second-rate version of somebody else" (Kennedy 1992, p.8).

It's cheesy but true. The lyrics of the record-breaking song "Greatest Love of All," written by Michael Masser and Linda Creed and then recorded by Whitney Houston in 1984, say **once you learn to love and accept yourself, no one can steal your dignity**. Pretty smart stuff for a pop song. After all, it was written by a woman who spent her entire childhood hungry, poor and ridiculed. She knew what she was writing about. So do I. It may sound old and tired—but until YOU like yourself, no one else will like you. **You must be the first one to see your own dignity, to respect yourself, if anyone else is to respect and like you, too.**

Dignity and Talking to Yourself: Internal Dialogues

Hello, I'm Jenny. I'm a word junkie. So forgive me a moment when I give you the etymology (history) of the word "dignity." It comes from the Latin word "dignus" which means worthy, and generally means deserving of esteem, praise, honor and respect. "Dignity" signals more, though. It has a feel of nobility, of grace, of confidence. It is part of you. You may be proud of an achievement or of an accomplishment. Well done. But unlike pride, dignity does not balance on one moment or one success. It is not fragile. It cannot be stolen on robbed, it can only be forgotten…by you.

To have dignity means first, that you will NOT cooperate with anything or anyone that humiliates you. Think about that, and read it again:

> **Having dignity means you will NOT cooperate with anything or anyone that humiliates you.**

Do you cooperate—maybe without realizing it—with people who hurt you, or tease you, or leave you out? If you buy the junk bullies say, if you look in the mirror and feed the lies back to yourself, then yes, you do. **You are helping those who misunderstand or mistreat you. You are bullying yourself. And there is no dignity in that.**

When you think about yourself, *what* do you think—privately? Are you mean to yourself? Are you kind to yourself? The words you hear are your **"internal dialogue,"** and you would not believe the power of that conversation. After all, who else is "talking" with you 24/7? Just you. You hear yourself A LOT.

It makes sense, then, that those thoughts you think about yourself are like computer programming codes. They shape your idea of you. **If you believe you are worthy and strong, you will live up to that truth. If you believe you are unworthy of love or happiness, you will live up to that truth, too.**

Consider your appearance, your school work, your intelligence, your talents, your social life. Do you think: why does everybody hate me? I'm such a geek. I hate my hair. I'm such a loser. That's **negative self-talk**. It's as if you are playing recordings of old insults in your mind, and while you're at it, you're convincing yourself that they are true. BUT:

Negative self-talk is almost always untrue!

Negative self-talk is a big, nasty bunch of misunderstandings, assumptions and exaggerations created by an NT world that doesn't quite "get" us. Sometimes, we're echoing back what we've heard said aloud. Other times, it's our own fears holding us back from taking a risk, from trying something new and a little bit scary.

So, if "I can't" really means "I won't," what is it that you *won't* do? Take a risk? Try? Face the chance of failing? **If you try something new or tough, I can't promise you won't make mistakes. But I can promise that if you won't try, you will never grow beyond who you are right now.**

Do you want to help the haters? The bullies? The doubters? I sure don't.

Catch yourself in the act of negative self-talk. Replace "can't" with a legitimate "can." And be on the lookout for **black-and-white thinking**! (Argh! That again?!?!) **Very little in life really is all or nothing, complete success or total failure.**

What we need is some **positive self-talk**—reminding yourself of simple, sincere truths like, "I'm a really loyal friend," or "I'm reliable and trustworthy." **Positive self-talk can also be a series of "combat thoughts,"** positive FACTS that are like antidotes to the negative self-talk poison.

Imagine that your negative talk is like a pothole dug along your path to dignity and self-respect. There you are, walking along, and suddenly, SPLAT! You trip in the hole and fall right on your face. So what do we have to do? We have to fill in the negative space and make your path smooth again. Enter the **"counter-thought!"**

> **Counter-thoughts motivate you, build your confidence and keep you focused on what you CAN control. They are specific responses to specific put-downs or doubts.**

Being Mindful: Stop, Listen, Replace

A thought is just a thought. It's no stronger than you allow it to be. Stop what you're doing, and take a close listen your self-talk. Write down what you hear, then write down and say OUT LOUD a positive counter-thought to fill in the "hole." For example:

The Negative Junk That Dug the Hole	Counter-Thought Fillers to Smooth Out Your Path
No one wants to be my friend.	I am a great friend. I can choose new people to approach.
I'm never going to pass that test.	I can ask for some extra help from the learning specialist.
I can't do anything right.	This is a chance to learn something new.

Why Does Any of This Matter Anyway?

Dignity is the reward you get for respecting the unique, precious person you are. Every person on the planet—NTs and Aspies alike—have the right to lead dignified lives. Do you give yourself that gift?

Do you show OTHERS and YOURSELF:

- honesty?
- kindness?
- tolerance for differences?
- trustworthiness?
- compassion?
- fairness?

When we refuse to bully ourselves, when we neither puff ourselves up nor tear ourselves down, we are dignified…and awfully attractive. Dating experts agree that **nothing is more appealing than confidence and dignity**. That's nice to know. But I say, forget Winning Others Over. Dignity is the key to winning over the MOST important person we will ever know—ourselves.

27

Likes, Tweets and Texts

Netiquette Need-to-Knows

Need-to-Knows

- Before you send a text or email to anyone, ask yourself: Is it true? Is it kind or good? Is it useful or necessary?

- People on the other side of the computer are real, with real feelings, real opinions and real reactions. However, the feelings, opinions and reactions they show online may not be real.

- What you write, text or post will ALWAYS be copy-and-pasteable, quotable, sharable and traceable.

- All "friends" are not all equal. Levels of friendship still exist in cyberspace.

- Avoid texting important conversations about the beginning or end of relationships, medical diagnoses or other major life events.

- Keep the amount of contacts when messaging, emailing, texting or posting balanced; reciprocity rules online, too.

Asperkid Logic

I'm going to completely date myself here, but whatever. When I was a kid (there I go, I've actually said it), the term "netiquette" didn't exist. Etiquette was what your mother made you read in Emily Post manners books, or you learned at "finishing school." There was no such thing as the Internet. But, thank goodness, I'm still young enough to say that my world swarmed with gadgets and passwords and social networks while I was still a single twenty-something. Which means I have had significant time to use the net to make certain things easier, and also to completely embarrass myself. (Yay.)

I have no doubt you have heard the basic warnings and rules of being smart and safe online. Please abide by them. People really do pretend to be kind, young and understanding—when they are, in truth, older, nightmarish and awful. So never, ever, ever give out your address, phone number or location to someone you don't know or in a public posting. Ever. My husband's a police officer, and he has seen bad stuff. Just trust me on this, folks. OK, enough said.

Mind Blind Online

The same social rules you've been reading all throughout this book are really the ones that you need to know online. Basically they break down to:

- impulse control impulse control impulse control (think before you send)
- being aware of the "you" that you create in others' minds
- knowing that invisible boundaries exist online, too
- "reciprocity" still rules.

When we allow our mind-blindness to kick in (which is, after all, our normal—so that means pretty often), we can get in the same trouble online that we do in the real world. Only it happens a LOT faster. Our world is interconnected by gadgets and apps and forums that offer nearly-instant contact and confusing relationships. We think we are level 5 friends with someone when actually, it's more like a level 2. Or a thoughtless text suddenly changes an actual level 4 friendship into a brand-new hater.

So, to begin, keep these points in mind at all times:

- People on the other side of the computer are real, with real feelings, real opinions and real reactions. However, the feelings, opinions and reactions they show online may not be real.
- Delete isn't ever complete. Online is forever.

"Like" Me: The Secret Rules of Social Networks

Social networks are awesome in lots of ways. They're great ways to connect with new (or old) friends, they help us avoid phone chit chat (yay!), and they're good for helping Aspies maintain relationships that we might otherwise neglect.

But they can also be a major pitfall zone. Boundary issues, over-sharing, levels of friendship—all the "invisibles" that we struggle with already—are EVERYWHERE, just waiting for us to step over lines and pop those dang social bubbles.

The key to surviving (and enjoying) Facebook, Twitter, LinkedIn, Tumblr, Pinterest and whatever site becomes hot next is to be THOUGHTFUL about everything you do in digital. Here's how:

- **Assume that anything you ever write will be misused or misunderstood.** That may sound a bit paranoid, but it'll keep you thinking. What would you want a bully, a boss, an admissions counselor or your future kids to be able to trace back to you? My grandfather, decades before the internet, had a line that still rings true: "Words that are spoken are thin as air. Words that are written are always there." What you say aloud can and will be repeated—sometimes correctly, other times, not so correctly. Either way, you can deny them or explain them. It's called "hearsay" when others report what they claim to have heard, and it's so wishy-washy that it's not even allowed in court. However, **what you write, text or post will ALWAYS be changeable** (hello, Photoshop?!), **copy-and-pasteable, quotable, sharable and traceable**.

- **Keep photos and usernames neutral.** College admissions officers, employers, your grandparents WILL see what you have online! You can look styled, casual, glamorous, cool, whatever—but if it's not a picture you'd be proud to show to Grandma, keep it off the computer. Even your username matters. No matter how funny or "hot" you think you look or sound, you don't; people who really are funny or attractive don't have to try to prove it or show it off. They just are.

- **Ask before you tag.** If you've been tagged (identified by name) in a photo and you don't want it linked to you, it's no problem for you to untag yourself. But don't put others in that position. When posting photos that include other people, avoid tagging them. Let them know the photos are up, and allow them to choose to tag (or not to tag) themselves.

- **Privacy settings are there for a reason.** Use them. Even then, though, assume that anything you post will be publicly viewable (after all, tablets, laptops and Smart Phones make even private screens portable). With the personal information that you do post—**be careful not to over-share** (typically Aspie danger zone). Other people don't want to read an autobiography; too much info just comes off as vain. Less is more. Those who get to know you will learn all they want to know.

- **The number of followers or friends you have does not equal your value as a person.** You can have 573 "friends" or 1000 followers, and not have a genuine friend in the whole group. Quality not quantity, remember? People who want to "collect" huge boatloads of "friends" aren't interested in relationships, they're interested in showing off.

- **All "friends" are not all equal.** Remember the levels of friendship? My online "friends" include people I hung out with in preschool but haven't seen since, my best friends in the world, and my make-up salesgirl. Obviously, they are not all at the same "level of friendship" in my life, but they are all in my newsfeed. Use Smart Lists to help you keep straight who is who, and who isn't an actual friend.

- **Friends of friends are OK.** It's fine to send a friend request to the friend of a friend, but accompany that with a little note so they can be sure you are who they think you are. Just because you remember someone doesn't mean she remembers you.

- **Too Much Information (TMI).** Before you post what you're wearing, eating or watching, ask yourself—"Would I care if someone else posted this?" If not, don't bother. Too many posts dilutes the posts that do matter.

- **The Wall is Reply All.** And, in email, Reply All is usually not good. It clogs people's inboxes and makes them less likely to pay attention to anything you have to say. Wall posts are like that; they cheapen you. Don't use the Wall to make plans with one person (or even a small group); you make others feel left out and come across as though you need everyone to know you have a social life. Use direct messaging for personal plans, praise or information.

- **Thumbs up or down.** You don't have to say yes to everyone who asks you on a date and you don't have to accept every friend request. "Ignore request" is a totally legitimate response if you really don't know someone or want a particular person messaging you. Or, if you break up with someone or find a particular "friend" to be embarrassing, hurtful or upsetting—

get rid of them. You are in charge of who you allow in your space, whether that's actual physical space or cyberspace. You don't have to leave room for negative people. "Un-friend" them for your own good.

Digital Decorum

Take a step out of social networks, and we still have a lot to keep straight with email and texting. Pop. There goes that danged bubble thing again.

For example? My understanding had been that if someone gave me their contact information, I could use it. Seems pretty logical, right? Only nothing in NT world is ever that easy. A year ago, our pediatrician gave me her personal email and cell phone number, because our daughter had a lot of medical issues going on. Well, one weekend, we ran into some trouble with another doctor, and I wasn't really sure how to handle it. So, I emailed our pediatrician. No reply. However, come Monday morning, she called me on the phone and proceeded to tell me how completely inappropriate I had been, that using her personal email was simply unacceptable. I thought I might vomit from humiliation. My voice barely squeaked out, "Oh, OK," and I felt myself go hot to the tips of my ears. I truly didn't understand what I'd done wrong—until I realized the familiar feeling: I'd crossed a boundary again. Ugh.

In another case, one of my kiddos' teachers asked me to please send her "all the information I had" about various testing we'd done. So I did. Literally. Then she went ahead and complained to the school principal that I had flooded her inbox with a ridiculous amount of emails. My literal interpretation was, apparently, the wrong way to take her request. And again, I was totally humiliated and lost as to what I'd done to upset her so much.

Secret Rules of Email

In thinking about those two incidents, I came up with my first **two secret rules of email**:

• **Invisible boundaries exist between personal and "professional" relationships; just because a professional**

person is friendly does not make him/her a friend. You can email friends and family, but only contact professionals (teachers, a boss, your therapist) at work and during business hours UNLESS it is a true emergency where someone's health or safety is in immediate danger.

* Multiple emails can make the receiver feel stalked or overwhelmed. **Be concise and to the point, combining multiple small emails into one, more complete note.** If you aren't sure what to include or not include in an email, ask the other person to specify EXACTLY what information he/she would like to have.

Beyond those…there are still more:

* **Watch your tone: go for clear not clever.** There's no way to make your tone of voice clear online, so people can easily misinterpret what you mean to say. For example, I have a really joking relationship with my father-in-law; we constantly tease about how he forgets to share news with the rest of the family. Last summer, I posted a message to the extended family, letting them know that we were coming into town for a week. I wanted to tell them myself, I wrote, because I wasn't sure we could trust Grandpa to spread the word (which would have been said with a wink and a laugh out loud). Unfortunately, some readers took my joke as an insult against the family's patriarch (luckily, he knew I was being completely good-natured); they read a tone that wasn't there. Online, that's not hard to do. So, be very clear in what you say, and if you think others may not "get" your humor, don't make the joke to start with. On the flip side, if you think an online comment sounds out-of-character for an otherwise nice person, ask about it—don't assume the worst. It's probably just a misunderstanding.

* **Don't forward, copy or attach a message without permission.** That's basically online gossiping.

* **Forwards are lame.** Don't send them. They annoy people. Period.

- **Be timely and thorough.** Reply within 24 hours, and make sure to answer all questions he or she may have asked you (even if that means saying that you don't know an answer). This is being respectful of everyone's time.

- **Get to the point.** People use email to save time, so try to keep yours short. Using bullet points also helps your reader see where attention is needed.

- **Spellcheck is there for a reason.** Everything you put out in the world is like an extension, or at least a reflection, of you. Sending notes that are full of spelling or grammatical mistakes sends the message that you don't care enough about the reader to take the time to check your work. But do beware of Autocorrect features! Failed "predictive corrections" have been known to send some VERY embarrassing replacement words.

- **It's all forward-able.** Anything you write can be cut and pasted or forwarded. If you don't want information out there in public, don't put it out there to start with.

TXT SVVY

I'm not going to reinvent the wheel, here, folks. You can read anywhere and everywhere about not texting at the table, while other people are talking, during a public performance, etc. What I want to emphasize to you is that **texting is the least personal type of communication there is—it's like interpersonal shorthand**. That's awesome if you just want to ask a friend to save you a seat in the movie theater. Not awesome if you want to break up with someone.

Avoid texting important conversations about the beginning or end of relationships, medical diagnoses or other major life events. It comes off as uncaring because it doesn't respect or include the other person in what should be a two-way conversation. Important talks should happen in person or, if absolutely necessary due to distance, over the phone—but never in texts.

Oh, and watch the ring tones. Keep them simple. Not everyone shares your humor or musical taste, and they shouldn't have to hear it.

How Much is Too Much?

Remember that whole reciprocity thing? Friendships and conversations are, we've said, like a tennis match or a teeter-totter. They have to be balanced to work. When one side overwhelms the other, it's no fun and an awfully short game. The same thing is true for digital communication.

While there's no hard and fast rule about the maximum number of texts, IMs, tweets or wall posts you can send to someone before you've officially gone from fun to creepy, look to the "level of friendship" to help you decide what to do. How often you can "safely" message without becoming a pest depends on how close your friendship is, how important the information is, and the time of day (I got an unimportant text at 6am today—not cool). Consider what it might feel like on the other side of your messages.

Imagine each new burst of messages you send as a new conversation. Check for reciprocity. Are you contacting this person about as much as she contacts you? Are you balancing the teeter totter? If you're overdoing it, the other person will feel annoyed quickly. Back off! Wait to be contacted before you send anything more.

On the other side, don't leave him hanging. If this is someone you like and want to keep as a friend (or more), be sure you are, in fact, replying to messages. Otherwise, it's as if you've walked away from the teeter totter and left your friend to fall flat on his bum.

Socrates Again

Do you remember the Socrates Triple-Filter Test? What goes for the spoken word also goes for the written word—maybe even more so. Therefore, if you don't remember anything that you've just read about netiquette, remember impulse control. Wait!!! Before you send anything to anyone, ask yourself: Is it true? Is it kind or good? Is it useful or necessary? If it passes the filters, go ahead. Otherwise, hit delete, and refresh your mind.

28

The Loveliest Curve
and an Open Door

Beauty and Chivalry are Alive and Well

Need-to-Knows

- To the right girl or guy, your quirky self is the most attractive person in the world.

- No guy or girl is worth crying over. And the one who is won't make you cry.

- Nothing is more attractive than confidence, courtesy and self-respect.

- "Beautiful" and "hot" are NOT the same thing.

- Being a "lady" means having self-respect and confidence.

- Being a "gentleman" means having common sense and good manners.

Asperkid Logic

My dad had a line that absolutely ticked me off every time he said it. Although, being an Aspie himself, I'm pretty sure he didn't notice that. Anyway, more than any other reprimand he could toss my way, "That's not very ladylike" was the most aggravating of them all. Was I supposed to cross my ankles and lift my pinkie? I was going to be a woman of the twenty-first century, after all. "Ladylike" sounded awfully old-fashioned and maybe even offensive, if you asked me.

Of course, he didn't ask me, and neither did anyone else. Which, apparently, turned out to be a very good thing, because (as in many other times in my life), I was being very loudly, very boldly—wrong. I'll get back to this.

Fast forward to college, when I briefly dated a really nice guy from outside of New Orleans, Louisiana—that's the "Deep South" for those of you not familiar with the United States. While I've now lived in the American South for my entire adult life, his "old-fashioned" manners were so much a part of him and his culture—and so different than what I was used to—that they made a real impression. He held doors open for me, held up my coat to make it easier to get on, that sort of thing. It was old-school, yes, and in fact, I remember telling him that I so appreciated his being a "gentleman." Though the word was as "old-fashioned" as "lady," we both knew I meant it as a compliment. And he took it as such.

Weird. As a child, I'd rebelled against the word "lady," yet here I was pleased to know a gentleman. Well, the world is full of ever-changing social labels and rules. What a word meant fifty years ago isn't necessarily what it means now. Like society, words evolve and change. And while the words "lady and gentlemen" probably sound as dusty to you as they did to me, the truth is that **the NT** world (and quite a few Aspies) adores people who **ARE ladies and gentlemen. Why? Ladies and gentleman of ANY age are people whose behavior is centered around courtesy, dignity and sincerity.** Rather nice qualities, those.

Girls, you may think your goal is for guys to think of you as "hot." **Guys**, you may think that no matter what, girls will only ever choose the jerk over the nice guy. This rule is about why you're both wrong. **Nothing is more attractive than confidence, courtesy and self-respect.** And, even if we ARE confident, courteous and respect ourselves, how do we show it to everyone else? I'm so glad you asked. Let's talk. Ladies first.

ASPERGIRL to ASPERGIRL: Short Skirts and Fruit Loops

When I was in high school, I was cast as the lead in the musical *Damn Yankees*. My part, Lola, was a vamp—"Whatever Lola Wants, Lola Gets," by means of "A Little Brains, A Little Talent" with the emphasis on the "talent." And Lola's talent was winning men. She was—and therefore I had to be—"hot." Dancing and singing about in front of 1000 people a night, I stripped down to fishnets and lace. "Dictionary Brain" had shaken up the scene, indeed. And it made quite an impression on the student body.

It also made quite an impression on me. In the span of one weekend, I literally went from having almost no social life to feeling like the honeypot surrounded by awfully hungry bees. Boys were everywhere. Calling, flirting. Walking me here or driving me there. There were party invitations every weekend. It felt like I was Alice through the looking glass, and I did NOT want to leave.

But fellow Aspergirls, I learned that when you are put up on a pedestal, you can get knocked down fast. No one looks you in the eye as an equal when you're up there. They look at you like an object. And every object is disposable. Which is why it annoys me to no end that the world now uses the word "hot" to mean "beautiful." They are NOT the same thing, and the difference between them is where I got very lost. And very hurt.

In the simplest of terms, the "hot" girl is the one all the boys are staring at. The "beautiful" girl is the one all the girls are staring at. The "hot" girl needs attention, and gets it. She will be "hit on" and approached by lots of guys. The "beautiful" one may not be—she can intimidate insecure people. She's intelligent, she is kind, she's confident in who she is, and she seeks the beauty in other people.

Learn to be her by learning to be the best you. How?

Keep looking yourself in the eye, improving what you want to improve, and reminding yourself that you are here for an unique purpose which no one else can fill. **We Aspergirls are Fruit Loops in a world full of Cheerios. We make life more colorful for everyone.**

I want you to grow into a beautiful "lady"—not an old fogy. An independent, compassionate, stylish chick who is authentic, but not perfect. Be good to your friends, good to whomever you love, good to your family, and always good to yourself. You will succeed and stumble over many things in your life. Do both with grace (not volume), humility (not showing off), and the NT truth that your behavior affects other people. That's why *how* **you succeed and stumble will determine the way the world treats you**.

A "lady" is made by how she chooses to behave. Because how you behave is entirely your choice, you get to choose to be a lady...or not. Will you take the time to say please, thank you, and I'm sorry even to people who "don't matter"? Will you be generous and realize that there is *always* something to be thankful for? Will you take care to keep your body healthy, your vocabulary creative, and your mind curious?

Aim now to become a "lady" later. An "Asperlady." Be inspiring. Be courteous and respectful in the ways NTs expect you to be (which is everything you've just read about in this book!). Show that you will speak up for yourself, are gracious, honest, fair and dignified ("WOO!"). And what else?

- **Study.** Educated people get to make things happen. Work hard and learn as much as you can (just remember to share it little bits at a time).

- Your loveliest curve is your **smile**. Wear it often. Show it off.

- Boys make GREAT friends.

- Remember: **Hygeia** and **Aphrodite** were BFFs for a reason.

- **Swearing** is for those who are not creative enough to express themselves well.

- Styles change. Bodies are different shapes. **Some looks are ALWAYS classic**: well-tailored, neutral colors (plus black) in natural fibers (like cotton) are great basics. You can jazz things up from there with whatever accessories make you *you*.

- There are very subtle differences (soooo hard for Aspergirls to see!) between confident, questionable, and trashy. Don't walk the line. **Leave a little something to the imagination. Go for "beautiful" over "hot."** As one male friend of mine put it, the more clothes a girl has on when she meets a guy directly equals how long he imagines the relationship. Showing everything at once doesn't say "confident chick" it says "insecure, desperate object." That's how you win attention, but it's NOT how you win hearts.

- **In make-up and in clothing, choose one feature to emphasize at a time. Make-up:** strong eyes or lips, not both. **Clothes:** spotlight a bit of one part of you. Pair a short skirt with long sleeves, or choose a more fitted top with jeans or khakis.

- If you aren't sure what to wear to an event, **ask** the host.

- **Guys are people, too.** If you are asked out (which takes major guts!) by someone you don't want to date, you don't have to go. But do have the courtesy to say so rather than avoiding him or lying. That's just mean. "I'm sorry, I just don't think we're a match," is a perfectly polite answer.

- Remember: no boy is worth crying over. And the one who is won't make you cry.

Humbly own your successes AND your blunders. You don't need to brag, and you don't need to beat yourself up. You need only to get into a habit of telling yourself out loud, every day that, **"I am beautiful. And I am enough."**

HEY, YOU GUYS! Manly Men

I realize that I am a bit biased, but I happen to think my husband is a total hunk. He's handsome, strong and smart. He's a guy's guy. AND, he's also a complete gentleman. I tell you this right away, guys, in case for one minute you think being a "gentleman" is, well, being a prissy loser. Wrong. It also doesn't mean being a "nice guy" who lets everyone walk all over him.

Being a "gentleman" means having common sense and good manners. It means acting in a way which other guys respect and, quite frankly, girls will love. Primarily you do it by being **honest, trustworthy (very Aspie!) and respectful**. That's where your **active listening and flexible thinking skills** come in (reread "Mirror! Mirror!" and "Broken Spaghetti," mini-chapters 9 and 11, for refreshers). After all, people respect those who respect them.

Why be a gentleman? What's in this for you? OK, I'm going to cut to the chase. It'll earn you money and win the ladies. **Men who learn to be gentlemen will go further in whatever careers they choose and are more attractive to women** (I know. I am one).

Your goal is to make other people feel comfortable around you—which is tough if you're not too comfortable around other people. But don't worry. You don't have to be Mr. Smooth. You just have to use the **conversation tools** we've already covered:

+ make eye contact if you are comfortable

+ use his/her name (it shows you are paying attention and sets others at ease)

+ ask questions rather than talking about yourself or your interests

+ introduce yourself (don't wait for the other person to start)

+ skip the swearing—it doesn't make you sound cool, it makes you sound dumb.

And there's one more really important thing: **chivalry**.

You Mean Like Knights?

When I say chivalry, if you know the word at all, you probably think of the Knights of the Round Table or something along those lines. Guys, I am not telling you to go out and get yourself a chain-mail suit of armor. Chivalry, as I would define it, is at the core of how you interact with girls and women. This is the stuff I picked up on in college, and what drew me to my husband. **Chivalry is understanding that women are equal to men in intellect and ability, but recognizing that we are not, in fact, men.**

What you like about girls is most probably what sets them apart from you. Their shape, their voice, even their smell. We are, after all, different from you. Personally, I very much like being a girl. I have no doubt that I am as smart or capable (or brave) as any male I've ever met. So, to me and to many girls, acts of chivalry feel like little "kindness gifts." You're showing **respectful appreciation for femininity**—that is, for girls and women and all we are and can do. For example? Well, there are lots, but some **good basics** are:

- Open doors for a girl (including the car door, which you should close after she's seated).

- Walk *beside* her when going up a flight stairs, not *behind* her.

- Walk along the street's edge if you are walking together.

- Offer your seat if a girl (or an older person) comes to a table or a room that is full.

- Always offer to see a girl safely home (whether by driving or walking her there).

- Help her put on her coat.

- Introduce her by name to any acquaintances you see when out together.

- Offer her your coat if it's cold and she doesn't have one.

- Never kiss and tell, and never believe the stories of guys who do.

In fairness, some girls may feel challenged by gestures you mean to be gentlemanly. No worries. Just respect the opinion of someone who doesn't seem to want a door held or refuses when you offer your seat.

Now, while I do know what it's like to be an Aspie, and a girl, I don't know what it's like to be an Asperguy. Conveniently, however, I happen to be married to one. My husband, John, is good-looking and friendly, but he was painfully shy growing up and absolutely terrified of girls. Mostly, he says, that was because he had no idea what was going on in their minds and was absolutely terrified of rejection.

Time has given him perspective, though, so I decided to do a little Q&A. I asked him to imagine being able to sit at a table and talk with his teenaged self. What would he, as an adult Asperguy, most want to let his younger self know? Here's what he said…

John's Turn: The Asperguy's Inside Perspective

- I could never understand the pretty girl with the jerk-of-a-guy phenomenon. Looking back on it, I did a lot of complaining about it but I never did anything about it. **I never asked.** A lot of times, the nice guys get passed over because they don't ask.

- You can't control whether a girl says yes to a date, and you have no real idea of why she might say no. Your goal has to be **getting up the nerve to ask** in the first place. That's the only thing you can control. And she can't say yes if you don't ask in the first place.

- Before you ask a girl out, **you have to have some type of rapport**—some conversation beyond just an introduction. Otherwise, you come off as weird or scary, and no girl is going to say yes to a date with someone she doesn't feel comfortable with.

- **Girls like it when you plan dates.** I didn't realize that and ended up looking unprepared when I meant to be easy-going. (Jennifer here: Before you go on a date, plan the evening—make a reservation, know the movie times. This shows you've put thought into the date, and that the girl matters to you.)

- **She can't read your mind.** She doesn't know what compliments you may have in your mind unless you say them out loud. She also doesn't know if something's bothering you unless you say so.

- **Don't kiss and tell.** What happens between the two of you stays between the two of you. Do not discuss her feelings with your friends, either. She's telling you in confidence, so keep it quiet.

- Girls are people, too. Even though you may find her beautiful, she may not think it of herself. She's a person, just like you, with her own insecurities. Even if you have butterflies at the thought of her, **no one is too out of reach to at least TALK to**.

- Just be yourself, and everything really does **turn out for the best**.

And keep in mind the **grooming tips** we've already covered. Dress for the occasion, and keep the cologne to a minimum. Oh, and though it seems weird, just trust me—pay attention to your shoes. They matter a lot more to girls than you realize. Ask a sales girl at a store like J.Crew or Abercrombie and Fitch to help you put together outfits (and shoes!), and while you're at it, show off the gentleman you know you are.

Last: guys, a beautiful girl doesn't need another admirer. She wants to be around people who see her as an equal, not as an object. And most importantly, she has to find something beautiful about you. So be your true, quirky self. To the right girl, that's the most attractive guy she'll ever meet.

29

There's More for Dinner than Mashed Potatoes

Missing the Bigger Picture

Need-to-Knows

* Aspies see beauty in pieces and parts; NTs prefer to focus on the total picture.
* The NT world expects us to get the "big idea" or "gestalt."

- Active Listening Skills ("Mirror! Mirror!") and Signal Words help you hear someone's main idea.

- "Palm Reading" can help you find the main idea in anything written.

- You must be able to accurately take information in to be able to support your own ideas and opinions.

Asperkid Logic

My favorite holiday is Thanksgiving. In the United States, Thanksgiving is about a month before Christmas, and it's really the official kick-off to the winter season. The purpose of Thanksgiving is—obviously—to give thanks for the blessings in our lives. But let's be honest, the real focus of the day is Thanksgiving Dinner. When you're young, you may get stuck at the "kids' table" with cousins you barely know and maybe an annoying sibling or two—but none of that really matters once the plates start filling with the most scrumptious feast of the year. Candied sweet potatoes and cornbread dressing, mashed, buttery potatoes, cranberry sauce, warm rolls, roast turkey, green beans, secret casserole recipes that only come out once a year…only to be followed by fruit pies and chocolate cakes, spiced cider, and the season's first Christmas cookies. It's a feast for the eyes, the nose and the mouth.

Warning: I'm about to sound like an English teacher for just a second (I was, so I guess it's not too much of a stretch), but don't worry. It'll be over quickly. What would you say was the topic of the paragraph you just read? You'd probably not have too much trouble agreeing that I was talking about Thanksgiving. And you'd be right.

OK, next question: what was the main idea? Now that—for some Aspies—is quite a bit harder. We'll get back to this.

When we are first being diagnosed, one of the "Aspie traits" psychologists look for is a fascination with "parts" of things, rather than with the "whole thing." So for instance, an Asperkid might be absolutely intrigued by the way an axel and wheel work together to make the tires spin, but not have much interest at all in making up imaginary play with a bunch of toy cars. An Aspie might be amazed at the way individual notes or musical rhythms function, or by interlocking hundreds of Legos, or fitting together complex jigsaw puzzles, unraveling grammar and word functions, or cataloging individual chemical elements.

We Aspies see beauty in those pieces and patterns. They're hypnotic and ordered. They are beautiful in their simplicity, and also in their complexity. It's no wonder we can get lost for hours in all of those pieces. Sometimes I feel sorry for NTs. They really don't appreciate how many patterns, connections and rhythms they miss by focusing on bigger ideas.

Actually, NTs see our interest in parts as somewhat troubling. They say that getting lost in pieces causes us to miss the "bigger picture" or point (they'd say "gestalt"). That makes some sense. **If we focus all of our attention on ingredients, we have less time or energy to look at a whole idea or thing.**

That's why I don't believe one perspective is better than the other. It's like looking at a mosaic. Up close (a la Aspie), the tiny tiles are beautiful in themselves. Step back (NT-ish), and the pictures those tiles make all together is amazing. Both ways of seeing are valuable.

Since this book is for us, though, let me tell you what NTs see and how we have to use that "inside information." **The NT world expects us to see the "big picture" and react to it as they would.**

Nurse Sharks and Mashed Potatoes

Several years ago, I sat in and listened while my daughter (Aspergirl!) did a listening comprehension test. That day, the speech therapist read aloud a whole paragraph. Nurse sharks, we heard, ate such and such, they lived somewhere, had this particular kind of body shape...and on and on with lots of information about these fish. Then she asked my Aspergirl what the reading had been about. And—with almost perfect recall—this kiddo repeated back the entire paragraph.

She got a perfect score on that test—but she shouldn't have. It was like hearing a voice recorder playing back what she'd heard, but she never really put the pieces together. She never really did add up those details (or "parts") to see the "total" topic: nurse sharks.

On another occasion, an Asperkid student of mine took a quiz that involved being able to explain why certain situations were ridiculous. This student was right—it was silly to say that someone had ice-skated across the Atlantic Ocean. She argued it was maybe possible over the Arctic Ocean, but not the Atlantic, which never froze solid. That seemed like a great answer to me. Until the psychologist who'd given the test pointed out that the "silly" part of the question wasn't which ocean was mentioned, it was that people don't generally ice-skate across ANY ocean. Oops. Missed that. I was too caught up in the details myself to realize that both the student AND I had overlooked the main point.

You know the expression, "getting right to the heart of the matter?" It means to be able to zero in on the main point someone else wants to communicate. To understand exactly what is most important in their message, putting aside any "extra pieces." **You could say that instead of getting right to the heart of the matter, we Aspies get right to the toenail. A detail or piece catches our attention, and we can't let go.** To us, that "part" of the larger story or idea is what we are meant to take away from the conversation. Except to the NT talking (or writing), we've gotten lost on an unimportant detail and missed the point. The result is that **the speaker feels unheard (and gets frustrated or sad), or we waste our time and energy on information that wasn't even important**. And that can mess up relationships and school work—fast.

Which brings us back to that Thanksgiving dinner table. It's a great visual. There's an endless buffet of splenderific food before us…but we don't see a feast. We just see the bowl of mashed potatoes. And you'd have to agree, there's a whole lot more for dinner than mashed potatoes.

Finding the Heart and Not the Toenail

Information is going to be communicated to you in one of two ways: either in writing (so you take it in by reading), or in speech (you take it in by listening).

To get an idea from one person's head into yours, a lot has to happen. He (1) has to know what he wants to get across, then (2) has to carefully, clearly choose words that match the ideas or feelings he has. Next, you have to listen (3) to what's being said (hopefully not getting too distracted in the meanwhile), and then interpret the words you've heard (4). It's at least a four-step process, and that's if nobody gets confused along the way. And even then, you haven't yet reacted to what's been said. No wonder this is all so confusing!

So what can you do to **find the main idea**—the "Thanksgiving feast" or "heart of the matter"?

- **When talking with friends or family:** use your **active listening skills**. They will help ensure that what you are understanding matches what the speaker means to get across. **Check in** along the way.

- Go back and **reread "Mirror! Mirror!"** (mini-chapter 9) for a refresher. Then practice—often.

- **At school:** write down whatever comes next when your teacher:
  - repeats information
  - writes information on the board
  - breaks down an idea into steps
  - contrasts pros/cons
  - sounds louder.

- Listen for **Signal Words**. These are words or phrases you'll often hear in school which act like the flashing lights at railroad crossings. They tell you to, "Stop! Look! Listen!" Something important is coming.

Type of Signal Word	Examples	What It Should Do
Introductory	Today, we'll be talking about... By the end of today, you should know...	Give you a general idea of the topic
Qualifying	However... Still... Although...	Point out exceptions to the usual rule or pattern
Cause/Effect	Because of...(blank) As a result...	Explain the connection between ideas or events
Compare/Contrast	On the other hand... Instead... Likewise... Yet...	Show the similarities and differences between ideas, events or things
Examples	For example... For instance... ...such as...	Give illustration; offer details that support or prove the larger point
Repeated or Emphasized	In other words... Again... Above all...	Rephrase information and repeat it; this tells you the information is important—may be the main idea!
Test Clues	Remember! Take note... You WILL see this again...	This is how teachers make spoken words sound bold to point out possible test questions
Summary	All things considered... In the end... Finally...	Wrap up the talk

+ **When reading (anything!):** "Palm Reading" is a technique you can use to help you find the main idea of anything you read. Imagine your hand is the information the other person is trying to communicate. You can even trace your hand on a blank piece of paper so you can actually *see* what you're doing. Then, use this "handy dandy" information organizer (sorry, couldn't help it). Remember: it doesn't have to be pretty or perfect—this is for your eyes only.

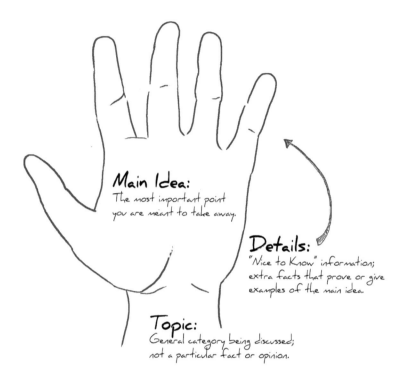

Main Idea:
The most important point you are meant to take away.

Details:
"Nice to Know" information; extra facts that prove or give examples of the main idea.

Topic:
General category being discussed; not a particular fact or opinion.

Want to practice "Palm Reading"? Let's try with my opening paragraph. What word or general subject do you see mentioned over and over? "Thanksgiving." That's the topic—the broad theme.

The **main idea is the most important point** the writer wants to get across—more than anything else. Everything else points to this idea. We put it in "the palm of your hand" to remind you that the main idea is central to the message you're meant to understand.

If you're not sure yet about the main idea…look for the "details," the pieces of information that work together to paint a picture. In this case, notice how there's a list (with LOTS of adjectives) of all sorts of foods I associate with Thanksgiving. There's also a mention of the tables, and the courses. Hmmm… so, if the foods (like pies and mashed potatoes and turkey), tables and plates are the details, then…

There it is! The main idea: "the real focus of the day is Thanksgiving Dinner."

Can we defend that answer? No problem. Our main idea is related to the topic (Thanksgiving), and the small pieces of evidence (the details about the different foods, seating and filling your plate) all support the opinion that the meal is the center of Thanksgiving.

So?

This book isn't about schoolwork. And we didn't just spend pages on "main idea" because it's tested more than any other skill at school (although that is worth noting).

We did this because **the world is trying to talk with you**. Whether you listen to a friend who is upset, a teacher before a test, or a new movie—you need to understand the point of what's being said. Whether you read my book, your favorite graphic novel or Shakespeare—you need to be able to scrunch all the words and ideas down into one important point.

Why? Because you don't have to agree with other people's points, arguments or ideas. You have your own voice. Your own opinions and experiences. And you have *every* right to have them. BUT.

We are entitled to our own opinions, but not our own facts. **The NT world will only listen to what you have to say if you can support your ideas with evidence.**

How do you do that? By getting the main idea. By taking information in and filtering it through your own mind. **Whether you are listening to a song or reading an encyclopedia, you have to accurately get other people's knowledge into your brain.** You have to figure out when they say something important and forget what's not. You have to think about what you learn, question it, and finally, make up your own mind. That's why you're here in the first place.

30

Wedgies, Tattletales and Queen Bees

Taking Your Power Back from Bullies

Need-to-Knows

- Aspies are prime targets for bullies because we are different and often defenseless.

- Tattling is meant to get someone in trouble. Telling is meant to get someone help (including yourself).

- You are only in charge of what YOU do. Unless someone could get hurt or is being bullied, don't be the "police officer."

- Bullying is about taking your POWER away. Telling is about taking it back.

- Bullying among girls is really complicated. Aspergirls and their families should read *Queen Bees and Wannabes* to understand the roles girls play in NT cliques.

Asperkid Logic

Let's cut right to the chase. Happy people don't need to hurt others. Bullies do. They are not happy people. They're cowards who prey on people with kind hearts and few defenses. Looking back at my own life, it turns out that every bully I ever knew had a lot of hurt of her own. They each looked for ways to take that pain out on easy targets. Like me. No, I won't ever excuse them. But I do feel really sorry for them.

I wish I could tell you that bullying ends after junior high or at some magic age. It doesn't, though. As long as there are sad people, people who are scared by what they don't understand or jealous of what they don't have, there will be bullies. And as long as we, Aspies, are different than the "typical" folk (forever), we will get targeted or taken advantage of. Which is why I want you to know what to do about bullies. Now.

Tattling Versus Telling: How to Tell Which is Which

If you've ever watched the TV show, *Phineas and Ferb* (a personal favorite of mine), you know that Candace—the big sister who is intent on busting her younger brothers—is a killjoy. While the boys fill their summer days inventing outrageously fun contraptions (like building the world's largest bowling ball or tallest zip-line), Candace fills hers figuring out how to get them in trouble.

Is she tattling or telling? No one wants to be called a tattletale, so how do you know the difference? Easy. It comes down to motivation. In other words, what do you want? Do you want to bust someone (a la Candace) or do you really need help? It's really pretty simple:

Tattling is meant to get someone in trouble.

Telling is meant to get someone help (including yourself!).

However...

Aspie pitfall alert! We like rules—they keep the world feeling more organized. We like for EVERYONE to follow the rules ALL the time. Trouble is, they don't. And other people don't want you to tell them how to behave. Even if you don't mean it that way, when you report peers who are breaking rules but aren't hurting anyone, they *will* see you as a tattletale. **Remember this: don't try to control anyone else. You are only in charge of what YOU do.** Unless someone could get hurt or is being bullied (see below), don't be the "police officer." Let an adult be the authority.

Bullying is about POWER. About getting it and about holding on to it. **Telling is about taking back your power.** It's teaching the world how to treat you.

Bullies use power to keep you (and other kids) quiet. Whether it's the thug dunking heads in the boys' room or the girl in control of everyone's party guest lists, bullies depend on bystanders to do nothing. They will call names like "snitch," or threaten anyone who gets in the middle of things. Most of the time, people will play along. But they shouldn't. And neither should you. As long as kids don't know the difference between telling and tattling, or aren't brave enough to speak up, the bullies get to stay in charge.

So what's not OK? Bullying includes:

- teasing, name-calling, put-downs
- shoving, punching, wedgies

- threats (of any kind)
- telling lies, secrets or spreading gossip (in person or online)
- stealing your belongings
- exclusion (leaving people out, telling others *not* to be friends with someone).

Bullying is on purpose.

Bullies do their dirty work where they won't get caught.

They expect their victim—and other kids watching—to be too intimidated to tell an adult.

Surprise them. Do something.

OK—But What *do* I do?

Let's start with what you don't do. Don't believe what other people say about you. The people who know the least about you always have the most to say.

And, as one of my favorite Pinterest pins says, "Don't try to win over the haters. You are not the jerk whisperer."

Now then, for what you *should* do. When someone is rude to your face, the best first defense is to stay cool. Their goal is to upset you, so don't let it show. **Look straight at them…hold it (without a reaction)…then look away and continue on with whatever you were doing or saying.** You've sent the message that you heard but have no intention of dignifying the comment, AND you haven't done anything to jack up the stakes.

However: if the behavior continues or if you are in physical danger, it's time to change the power dynamics NOW.

Review your self-advocacy skills ("Standing Up Straight," mini-chapter 25). Choose an adult you trust, and get some help. Oh—and by the way, the old "ignore them and they will go away" answer doesn't work. At least not for very long. That's the line our parents taught us, so an adult may repeat it to you. In that case, ask for another idea (say "Or what else could I try?") or go to an adult at school.

Above all, remember: this is your world, too. Maya Angelou, the poet, said, "I can be changed by what happens to me, but I refuse to be reduced by it." **You get to be the hero in your own life story.** Now go out and find yourself some justice.

A Little Extra Note, Aspergirl-to-Aspergirl: Cliques and Queen Bees

Bullying among guys is usually a lot easier to see because it's physical. But you and I both know that **female relationships are incredibly complicated**. So if we, as Aspergirls, are starting off at a disadvantage socially, the idea of being able to skillfully detect "frenemies" or "cattiness" is just unfair. It'd be like asking a deaf person not only to listen to music, but also to memorize the tune and start playing along. It just isn't going to happen.

Imagine you were to pick up a novel you've never read. Turn to a random page, and get really close, making a telescope out of your fingers so all you could see was a single letter or maybe a word. OK, now: give me a plot summary. What? How are you supposed to tell me what happens if you can't see anything except the little spot in front of you?!

Exactly. You are too close to the world of BFFs and "break-ups," the sleepovers and the drama to get a good look at what's happening around you. I'm over a decade out from teenager-hood, though, and I can see better from here. So I am going to have to ask you to trust me, because, sad as it is, none of this drama goes away when you turn twenty.

Want my credentials before you trust me? Done. I'm an Aspergirl, like you, and I know what it's like to desperately want to fit in. I know what it is to try to get your jeans just right (but hate the feel of denim), or to think you've made a friend only to turn around and have her making fun of you right behind your back. I have starved myself to fainting, found myself in dangerous circumstances with boys I didn't trust and have let my entire idea of who I was be decided by other people. I've also turned out quite well, thank you. Men seem to think I'm easy on the eyes, and women think I'm fun. Those are very nice compliments. But they don't define me any more than the insults did long ago. Nope. I've finally figured out that I—that WE—aren't "weird." We're eccentric and FABULOUS.

You, my fellow Aspergirls, are not alone. I'm in it alongside you, and am awfully proud to be there. Have faith that what I tell you is my best stuff—the same perspectives I offer my Asper-daughter (she even chooses to listen sometimes). When it comes to figuring out the craziness of girl-world, I want you to find an adult you love. This can be anyone: your mom, your dad, an aunt, a counselor at school, it doesn't matter. And then, together, I want you to read a book called *Queen Bees and Wannabes* (by Rosalind Wiseman). There is, I discovered, a whole lot of crazy ridiculousness going on out there in NT Girl World; and we are just not hard-wired to get it.

In *Queen Bees and Wannabes*, Ms. Wiseman does to girls' friendships what we did earlier to friendships in general; she sorts out the levels and the "roles" that girls fall into. I cannot tell you how desperately I would have loved to have read this as a young Aspergirl. Yes, I knew there were "leaders" among the girls. I can even remember one girl who literally would lean her elbow on other girls' shoulders, as if they were objects, not people. It was humiliating, really. And yet, girls felt proud when she "used" them. But beyond identifying the "leader," I couldn't see any rhyme or reason. Maybe it's the same for you.

You may have heard that real bees communicate by dancing. Well, it seems that human "Queen Bees" have a routine, too, with choreographed roles and steps. The **Queen** uses charisma, looks and strategy to influence the ways other girls are "allowed" to interact. **She weakens girls and their relationships so she will feel stronger and remain important to everyone.**

Among the Queen Bee's "court" are: **sidekicks** (girls who want to take over as queen), **floaters** (have friends in different groups), **bystanders** (want to be nice but also really want to be included), **wannabe-messengers** (will do anything to be included, eventually get turned on), and **bankers** (appear harmless to adults, they trick you into trusting them) (Wiseman 2009, pp.86–91).

Cliques are complicated and confusing, subtle and always-changing. While they will never be the natural habitat of us Aspergirls, they are how most female groups work—no matter how old you are. We must learn how to find safe places and authentic friends. If we don't, we become **"the targets"** of NT girls and eventually, of boys, too. That's why you have to learn the structure of Queen Bees' Courts, and why you deserve help handling them.

Bullying doesn't have to leave bruises to break your heart. You, Aspergirl, are lovely and precious. And you are far too fabulous to let anyone else get in your way.

31

Through the Looking Glass

Laughing at Yourself without Being a Laughingstock

Need-to-Knows

- Laughing at your *mistake* is NOT the same as laughing at *you*.
- The NT world considers laughing at your own blunders to be one of the "highest" kinds of humor.

- An action may be funny. A person is not. The joke is what you did, it isn't who you are.

- Do not make fun of your own pain just so it's not so bad when others hurt you. It doesn't work and it costs you self-respect.

- NTs perceive those who can laugh at themselves as secure, confident, strong and likable.

- A person who isn't afraid to tease him or herself makes a connection with everyone listening.

- No one can laugh at you if you're already laughing.

Asperkid Logic

For most of human history, people have relied on polished stone or the still surface of a pond to see their own reflection. Almost 200,000 years of faces. And most of them would never see themselves. They would never see their own eyes or smile or chin. The little pieces of themselves that everyone else could see. It wasn't until less than 200 years ago that a common, affordable mirror was invented—taking the luxury item out of the hands of the rich and handing it over to the rest of the world. Suddenly, you could stare into your own eyes clearly. You could see, thanks to the mirror, that you had a face, a body, a self that was just as human as everyone else's.

Have you ever tried to catch your own eyes moving in a mirror? Of course you can't do it—but I know I've tried. It seems like the face you see is Someone Else, doesn't it? That you are "de-tached" (instead of attached) to him or her. That you aren't *really* one and the same. Yet there you are. A mind behind a face that's seen by everyone you meet. But what on earth does any of this have to do with laughing? Quite a lot actually.

Even little kids laugh at slapstick or physical comedy—why do you think potty humor and pies (etc.) in the face are so big in kids' movies? It's easy to "get" the silliness of whipped cream all over some guy's face. My two-year-old would laugh at that. Higher up the comedy chain, though, is the kind of laughter that comes at an unexpected situation, not at an action. Let me give you an example.

I was a college cheerleader. One season, our coach was having a particularly tough time getting the girls to practice on time. So, she made it known that anyone who was late to the next practice would have to sit out the next game—in full uniform, for everyone to see. Now, to that point, I'd not ever been late to a single practice. Still, I was not about to push my luck. The next time we were scheduled to work out, I made sure I went to dinner early so there'd be no worries about getting to the (rather far away) Athletic Center by the 6:30 start time. While I sat in the dining hall, leisurely eating my food, a friend of my teammate approached, and asked why I wasn't at practice. I looked up, but it was only 5:45. What was the rush?

The rush was that I was wrong. Practice was at 6pm, and at least a 20-minute walk away. And it was dark. And raining. And really cold. Dang. In seconds, I was out the door, jacket over my head for protection. Down the cobbled sidewalk I ran, dodging huddled students and there—like a beacon of hope—I saw ahead of me the headlight of the campus shuttle pulling up to its corner stop. If I made it, I'd get to practice on time. So I gave it everything I had, bolting for that van until I thought my lungs would burst. I reached the corner while the van was still idling, grabbed the handle, threw open the door, and tossed my sopping self in, gasping, "Athletic Center, please!" through stringy, wet hair. There was silence. And when I got the wet hair out of my eyes, I realized that the quiet was due to the complete and utter shock of the passengers around me. Apparently, the van I'd just entered wasn't, in fact, the university shuttle. It was just some poor, random family's car. And I, a strange, dripping, shouting cheerleader, had just thrown myself inside.

Stellar.

Yes, I was late for practice. But no, they didn't sit me out. The story was too hilarious.

Now: honesty check. Did you laugh just now? Or at least think the story was amusing? I really hope so, because that *is* one of my better embarrassing moment stories. And to our earlier point, the humor—the joke—is the unexpected situation. I (and you) did not expect the end to feature me seated in a stranger's minivan. The intended result didn't occur. There was an error, a failure, a mistake.

So, basically, you just laughed at my failure.

It's OK, though. Laughing at my *mistake* is NOT the same as laughing at *me*.

The NT world actually considers laughing at one's own blunders to be the "highest" kind of humor, because it requires that we step out from behind our own eyes and see ourselves as someone else would. It's like seeing "another" face when you gaze in the mirror. Or at a photo. Seeing yourself as just another person.

Truth: if you only see your own perspective, life is a lot less funny. If I only looked at the fact that I was wet, in a stranger's car AND late for practice, well, there's nothing funny in that! It's actually pretty miserable. If you look at it from the perspective of the people in the car, though, well, after they got over their shock, they laughed like crazy at the surprise. Even my cranky coach laughed when I arrived, dripping—but with a rather awesome story to tell. From their perspectives, this was really priceless.

Different perspectives reveal mistakes, absurd situations, shortcomings and flaws that are, well, funny. To see the humor, to laugh at ourselves, we have to step away from ourselves. You, after all, are not your mistakes.

Why Bother?

Seeing ourselves as the world sees us is hard—for NTs, and especially for Aspies. So, why bother? Why put in the effort to have a laugh at our own expense? Well, it's not really at our expense. That's sort of the key. We're not putting ourselves down or bullying ourselves. I'm just asking you to consider the silly surprise you might see if you looked at yourself from another person's perspective.

An action may be funny. A person is not.

The joke is what you did, it isn't who you are.

Taking life—or yourself—too seriously is no fun. It's also not going to serve you well in the NT world. Why? There are a couple of reasons:

- **Laughter is good for you.** It's healthy. It lowers your blood pressure and raises your spirits. And if you can laugh at yourself, you will never be without a source of amusement. After all, whenever you need a pick-me-up, you've always got you.

- **NTs see those who can laugh at themselves as secure, confident, strong and likable.** People who are insecure about themselves feel the need to impress everyone else, to brag, to puff themselves up. NO ONE likes to be around a show-off. Confident people, however, don't need to show off. They're already certain of their own worth, and don't need to prove anything to anyone.

- Laughing makes you relatable. **A person who isn't afraid to tease him or herself makes a connection with everyone listening.** Everyone has embarrassed themselves, failed at something or sounded foolish at one time or another. Everyone! When you use "self-effacing humor" (laughing at your own mistakes), you're showing that you are just like everyone else—you, too, know what it's like to mess up.

- **NTs want to know and be with relatable people.** They don't like insecure or stuck-up people. Actually, neither do many Aspies.

- **No one can laugh at you if you're already laughing.** If you trip and drop all of your books, people *will* laugh. It's unexpected, and in NT world, expected situations are either scary, "weird," or funny. If you are too concerned with looking "cool" or "perfect," you won't laugh if you trip. You'll feel embarrassed and get angry or frustrated. Then, the laughter will be *at* you. But if you accept your own blunders and laugh at your mistakes ('cause they may really be funny), the laughter can only be *with* you.

- **ANYTHING can be worse.** Take any mistake for what it is and nothing more.

So often, Aspies are told to "lighten up." To take life a little less seriously. And the truth is that the first thousand times or so that you hear that advice (especially after you've royally goofed), you probably have no interest whatsoever in taking a "step back" or seeing anything from anyone else's "side." If you are embarrassed or upset and feel that people are laughing at you, you probably don't and can't see how a situation could possibly be funny. But if you can "de-tach" yourself from the momentary discomfort—you may find yourself laughing away what would otherwise be the most embarrassing moments of your life.

From one Aspie to another, a bit of warning, though. Do not make fun of your own pain just so it's not so bad when others hurt you. That's bogus. It's a lie, and it doesn't work. A famous comedy actor, Alan Alda, said that you should "laugh at yourself, but don't ever aim your doubt at yourself." The kinds of relationships you want or need in NT world—with teachers, friends, dates, family—are based on respect. Turning yourself into the class clown only gets you laughed at; it doesn't earn respect. Remember: YOU are not the joke.

You know, I've noticed an odd thing. Often, after someone cries deeply, he will laugh. When someone laughs really hard, he will tear up. And sometimes, when sad feelings are too overwhelming, he may laugh at a completely inappropriate time. It seems to me that laughing and crying are awfully connected—our body's natural ways of handling strong feelings.

Imagine that the world is not full of crystal-clear mirrors, reflecting only our most serious selves. Maybe it's full of funhouse mirrors, showing us the silliness of other perspectives. Try to be like an observer, watching someone else doing what you've done. Is it funny? Honestly? Let the world see that we Aspies are, actually, not that different—that we aren't scared to mess up now and then. We don't think we're any better than anyone else, and we know we're not any worse. We know that our mistakes don't make us losers, they make us human. And, sometimes, they make us funny. So be real. Be relatable. Be you.

And laugh.

Stickies

(Little Nuggets of Aspie Truth—Sticky-Note-Sized)

1. If you want (or expect) something to happen, and it's not happening, speak up. Ask if you can help make it happen.

2. If you don't want something to happen, and it is happening, speak up. Ask someone you trust for help.

3. Advice is not an insult to your intelligence. It's just additional perspective you may (or may not) find useful.

4. No one knows what you want, need or like unless you say so. What is obvious to you isn't obvious to everyone else (and vice versa).

5. Even "excuse me" becomes an interruption if you keep saying it.

6. When a door opens, wait for other people to exit before you walk in.

7. Ask *how* others want to be helped rather than deciding what they need. Your good intentions may come off as cheeky or presumptuous if you don't.

8. Don't change the TV channel on the TV if other people are watching the show.

9. Same goes for music. Ask before you change anything in case someone else likes the song.

10. After getting off of the phone, share any news. No one else knows what was said on the phone unless you tell them.

11. Knock before opening a door. Wait to be told to come in. If it's closed, it's closed for a reason, and you need to respect others' privacy.

12. Use names (antecedents), not pronouns (he, she, it, they, etc.). "He has it" doesn't help listeners imagine what you

see in your mind. Say "Mike" or "Kevin" instead of "he" and "the phone" or "the ball" instead of "it."

13. If someone's body is busy, their mind probably is, too. Pick another time for any important conversations.

14. Flush.

15. Say what you need from someone, not what the problem is (try "Please move over a bit?" instead of "I can't see the TV." Or, "May I have a refill?" rather than, "I'm out of juice.").

16. Other people may be able to see you even if you don't see them.

17. Leaving on time is as important as arriving on time.

18. Hold the door for other people.

19. Say "Thank you" if someone holds the door for you.

20. If someone's whispering to you, they want to be private or discreet. Reply very quietly or shrug to show you don't understand. Don't answer or ask what they are saying loudly enough that everyone can hear.

21. Say "Excuse me" whenever good manners say you should— even if you think no one's listening.

22. "When are you leaving?" comes across better as, "How long will you be staying?"

23. Accidents really do happen. Sometimes, no one is to blame.

24. It is great when people you meet seem kind and welcoming. Remember, though: that's an acquaintance, not a friendship.

25. Only answer questions that are addressed to you.

26. Someone who tells other people's secrets will tell yours, too.

27. If you have to say, "Don't tell anyone this…" you shouldn't be telling them either.

28. If you wouldn't say it *to* someone, don't say it *about* someone.

29. Don't give away your power by letting one person's opinion affect your decision-making.

30. Paying people in change (with coins) can be insulting. It implies their services aren't worth much.

31. If you are going to be more than ten minutes late for an appointment, call right away. This shows value for the other person's time.

32. If you are planning to cancel an appointment (for a haircut, with a doctor, etc.), try your best to give at least 24 hours' notice so the time-slot can be filled, and the professional doesn't lose money.

33. Hold off before sending multiple emails. Try, if you can, to condense them into a single, thorough, bullet-pointed note. The recipient will prefer that to an inbox full of bits and pieces.

34. Try to match your volume to the volume of others who are speaking.

35. Check with your friend before asking his or her ex on a date.

36. Guys: in public bathrooms, leave at least one open spot between you and another dude, unless every "station" is taken.

37. Girls: "I'll call you" doesn't always mean he actually will.

38. Call or text before stopping by someone's house. Surprise visits can make people feel unsettled.

39. Being on-time is understood to mean that you are reliable and responsible. Being late communicates that you are disrespectful or disorganized.

40. Arrive about five minutes before you are meant to meet someone, but not more than ten minutes late.

41. Always address adults by their title (Dr. or Mr. so-and-so), unless they say otherwise.

42. In public places (like the movies or a restaurant) where room allows, choose a table or seat that is apart from others. Otherwise, they may feel that you are trying to intrude on their conversations.

43. When a friend spends time with other people, it doesn't mean you're no longer wanted. No one person can (or should) fill ALL the friendship needs of another.

44. Telephone messages should be brief and to the point—it's a message, not a conversation. Say who is calling, who you'd like to return the call, and how to get in touch with you.

45. Say "excuse me" if you need to get close to or move past someone, even if you're not actually touching them.

46. If you're not sure whether something you know is meant to be kept secret, don't share it.

47. Making a friend choose between you and another friend is a sure way to get "dumped."

48. Have a plan when a friend comes over to hang out. An activity (anything from baking cookies to building Legos) gives you something to talk about.

49. Wait to be invited. Asking to be invited to someone's house or party will make the other person feel pressured and uncomfortable.

50. You have two ears and one mouth. So, use that ratio in one-on-one conversations. Listen about two-thirds of the time. Talk about one-third of the time.

51. You can feel bored without showing it. Yawning while someone else is talking is disrespectful.

52. Rolling your eyes sends the message that you think you are "better" than the speaker.

53. Stay in the room if someone is speaking to you (even if you can hear from another room).

54. Ask how you can help rather than assuming you know what someone else would find most helpful.

55. If you feel angry, say so. It's OK to be angry. It's not OK to be violent, mean or hurtful. It's also not OK to swallow the anger—it'll only explode later.

56. Everyone passes gas. And other people DO notice, even if you don't think they have. So either excuse yourself to the restroom first (most polite), or say "pardon me," if it's already happened.

57. Give advice when someone asks you for it—but ONLY when you are asked for it. Otherwise it's being bossy.

58. Body changes, functions or troubles are best discussed in private (at home, with a doctor, parent, or friend you know well).

59. Give your best effort in all that you do. No matter what you are capable of, others think the work they see you do *is* the best you *can* do.

60. Bathroom garbage goes into the trash basket. Wrap anything personal, soiled or sticky in toilet tissue before disposing of it.

61. When waiting in line (queue), remember to leave "hula hoop" space between you and folks around you. Leave extra room at a pharmacy.

62. Use a disposable tissue to wipe the counter dry after washing your hands. It's unpleasant for the next person to come to a wet, messy sink.

63. Wash your toothpaste down the sink after you brush rather than leaving it to dry in the sink. People don't want to see something that's been in your mouth.

64. When you want someone's help, **go to him**. Don't call for (or wait for) him to come to you.

65. When borrowing something, treat it BETTER than if it were your own. Return it soon—without being asked, and make sure it is clean. If you've damaged the item at all, replace it.

66. Ask before touching things that belong to others—never assume they won't mind. Controlling yourself shows respect and good personal boundaries.

67. "But I was just…" or "But I just wanted…" isn't a reason for breaking a rule or not following directions. It's an excuse about to be disguised as a logical argument.

68. Feelings cannot be wrong, but the thoughts that lead to them can be (so you may feel upset, sad or worried without need). Feelings are adjectives: "I feel (blank)" (see the Feelings Chart on the next page!). An idea, thought or opinion could follow "I feel like/that…" Check that your ideas are accurate before you react.

69. "I" sentences go over better than "you" sentences. ("I don't mind sharing once a week" vs. "You borrow my stuff too often.")

70. Keep your hands outside your clothing and to yourself.

71. In a cafeteria, ask before sitting down. "Is this seat taken?" works just fine.

72. If two people's bodies are close together and their voices seem quiet, assume they are discussing something they want to keep private. Not a good time to jump in.

73. Study TV—especially shows on Disney that are meant for teens/tweens. Watch the way characters dress to get ideas of what's popular. Notice that they ask questions of each other to keep conversations going.

74. Just because something is the most important thing to you right now, doesn't mean it is the most important thing of all.

75. Don't wake someone who is sleeping because you have a question or need something. Wait until everyone is awake.

76. Speak, don't scream. No one listens to yelling. Everyone listens to whispers.

77. It's impolite to invite yourself to someone's house or party.

78. Leave drawers and cabinet doors closed, unless they are yours.

79. Very little in the world is actually "never" or "always." Try to avoid the words.

80. Before you speak or write, imagine the picture you want to make the other person see with your words. Give the information they need to "see" what you do (who, where, number, color, when).

81. Spacing off and thinking look alike. Say, "I'm thinking about what I want to say," if you need time, otherwise other people think you're not paying attention.

82. If you know you will need some else's help, give plenty of notice. They probably have other commitments besides helping you and can't drop everything else right away.

83. OHIO: Only Handle It Once. You have a lot to remember, and when you forget, you send the message that other people's feelings don't matter to you. Act. The first time you read an email, get a voicemail, or become aware of a task you have to do—DO something right away: Handle it now. Delete/trash it. Prioritize it to a "finish by" bulletin board and set a calendar alarm to remind you when it's due.

84. It's OK to not know, but it's not OK to not try.

85. Everything gets easier. I promise.

Practice Sessions

Now that you've read through the (Secret) Rule Book, it's time to see those NT expectations in action. You're about to watch six social situations unfold. Sometimes, things will go smoothly. Other times, different choices might've worked out better. Consider what decisions you'd make, and why.

As you read, you also want be sure to watch out for our three notorious Aspie pitfalls:

- mind-blindness (not considering other perspectives)
- impulsivity (talking or acting without thinking of the consequences)
- black-and-white, all-or-nothing thinking (AKA being uncooked spaghetti).

OK, fellow Aspies, I know you're ready for this. Sit back, watch what happens, and think about the options. Ask: what went well, what could've been better—and how will you handle the same kind of situations in your life?

#1 The Main Idea

Post-Game Wrap-Up: What went well, and what could've been better?

Good: The host greeted his guest at the door and invited her in—good start.

Needs Improvement: His correction about the "family members" wasn't necessary (triple-filter!) and may have even embarrassed his guest. More importantly, as the host, it is his job to introduce his mom and brother to his friend (and vice versa) by name, not to leave her to ask.

Also, if someone hasn't been in a place you know well (like your house), you should escort them clearly—never turn your back and let them feel lost. "Come along to the dining room with me, and then I could get you a drink if you'd like," would've made the guest feel certain where she should be and altogether welcome in an unfamiliar environment.

#2 Pick and Choose

Post-Game Wrap-Up: What went well, and what could've been better?

Good: Everything! The New Girl wanted to *choose* friends based on her *own* experiences with them, rather than what other people had to say. She took a big (but smart) risk. She publicly stuck up for someone who felt pretty badly about himself, and remembered that it's the quality—not the quantity—of friends we have that matters most.

Needs Improvement: Nothing. Except Her Royal Highness the Queen Bee's lousy attitude.

#3 Police Officer

Post-Game Wrap-Up: What went well, and what could've been better?

Good: This Asperchick cares about her activity, about showing respect for her instructor, and is working hard at what she does.

Needs Improvement: There is already an authority figure present; in the studio, it's the teacher. If other kids continue to goof off, he will (eventually) correct them. Aspergirl's job is to work on her moves, not to be the "police officer" and tell other kids what to do or not to do (which also tells the teacher she doesn't count on him to run the show).

If the bad behavior continues without being corrected, she'd have every right (self-advocacy) to go to the instructor after class—privately—and (without naming names) "speak in sandwiches" (see mini-chapter 15). Mention that their lessons mean so much to her, and that she has a hard time concentrating when other students goof off between drills. This way the teacher maintains his authority (and pride), the kids haven't been called out in public by a peer, and she gets the kind of class she deserves.

#4 Stood Up

Post-Game Wrap-Up: What went well, and what could've been better?

Good: A whole lot went right here! Both kids made plans with a friend ahead of time; they were also both honest with each other about their feelings (all kinds of feelings: anger, self-doubt, fear, frustration, relief, happiness). The result was that both friends had the chance to express themselves and be heard—she didn't jump to conclusions that her friend was trying to embarrass or ditch her, and talked TO her friend, not ABOUT her friend to others. In turn, he got a good lesson into how his behavior affects others. Then, a sincere apology was offered and accepted. This is GOOD stuff, not to mention a great reminder that "one mistake does not a friendship break."

Needs Improvement: Our buddy forgot that other people's plans might be depending on him. By neglecting to tell his friend that he'd changed his mind about going, he really messed up her evening. The key to any good relationship is communication. No one else knows what you want, think or feel unless you say so—and it's up to you to say so! After all, it's unfair for others to miss out or be inconvenienced because you haven't been clear or forthright (and vice versa).

#5 Busy Body

Post-Game Wrap-Up: What went well, and what could've been better?

Good: Our Aspie friend *did* ask for help—that's important.

Needs Improvement: Remember—a busy body means a busy mind. The teacher wasn't ignoring our friend, who certainly shouldn't give up on asking for help; Mr. Jones's body language (hands in hair) was saying he was frustrated and overwhelmed. Look around! There was a lot going on: shouting, fires, spills, explosions! Mr. Jones was really busy and probably never even heard the question about test tubes. This would have been a great time for Asperguy to ask someone else for help, keep looking for a solution on his own, or wait for things to calm down before adding any other demands for the teacher's attention.

#6 Sweet Melody

Post-Game Wrap-Up: What went well, and what could've been better?

Good: This Aspergirl recognized she was "catastrophizing." Before letting her thoughts and emotions run wild, she checked back in, reviewing what was *actually* said versus what her insecurities "heard." She knew she could trust her teacher—so it wasn't likely the suggestions were meant to be hurtful. They were meant to be helpful. Best of all, she even thanked her teacher for the constructive feedback and promised to use the suggestions to improve her work.

Needs Improvement: Nothing! Great job all around. With this attitude, this Aspie *will* be the "hit of the show."

Stick a Fork in It— We're Done

AKA The Conclusion

Ladies and Gentlemen, you've done it. From "Sticky Note" reminders to Asperkid Logic, *The (Secret) Book of Social Rules* can officially go in your "been there, read that" pile. But before you close the covers, I just have two more important stories to run by you.

The first has to do with one of my all-time favorite TV comedies, *The Big Bang Theory*. For those of you who haven't watched it (they have over 20 million Facebook fans), *Big Bang Theory* (BBT) has truly turned geek into chic. It's the story of four brilliant young research scientists, their love of super-heroes and technology, and total confusion at all things social. Suddenly, at least on TV, "quirky" is cool. Since BBT's debut, online creativity havens like Pinterest and Etsy have even begun to proudly feature "geekery" as a (crazy-popular) product category.

The show's most beloved character is the oh-so-obviously-Aspie, Dr. Sheldon Cooper. A 30-ish theoretical physicist, Sheldon is brilliant, has no concept of private/public information, proudly speaks fluent Klingon, wears only vintage super-hero T-shirts, has a designated "spot" where he MUST sit on the couch, is utterly confused by sarcasm, has anxiety attacks when his routine changes and doesn't understand social norms. Sound familiar to anyone? The best part of his Geeky Pride, though, is that the audience truly laughs *with* him—because we know (underneath his "rude" speech or lack of empathy) Sheldon's not a bad person. That's something I wish the world understood about *all* of us.

Last week, I was watching a BBT episode with my Asperhubbie—while sitting in my regular couch spot, eating my regular snack food—when, oddly, Sheldon began to offer his roommate some social advice. Sheldon explained that he had thought "typical people's" social behavior was without logic or reason, until he watched their interactions more closely. On anthropological study, he discovered that their behavior wasn't random—it was organized into regular patterns and governed by "non-optional social conventions." My husband burst out laughing. "Oh my goodness!" he shouted. "Sheldon read your Rule Book!"

I wish! The fact is, though, that we Aspies *do* need to have social patterns illustrated and explained to us. Heck, Sheldon even developed a scientific flowchart, called the "Friendship Algorithm," to make new friends. It's such a comic masterpiece that practically every T-shirt website now carries some version of the "Friendship Algorithm." Why tell you all of this? Two reasons. First, because as I promised, when you can take a step outside of your own perspective, we Aspies are darned funny people. So laugh along with the millions of others who adore Sheldon. And second, because if there weren't a whole lot of people out there just like you and me, do you honestly think there would be a primetime show about Aspie quirkiness or that it would be loved all over the world? No way. We, my fellow Aspies, may not be as typical, but we're far from alone.

There will be some days that you feel you are alone, though. I know. I understand. And that brings me to my second, and last, important story in this book. My dad, an Aspie, used to buy four or five greeting cards for every birthday or holiday— he couldn't express his emotions well, so he gathered enough of other people's pre-written words until they combined to form the bigger message he felt.

Feelings are tough for Aspies to nail down and communicate. In this NT world, we may talk and talk, but rarely do we feel understood. Enter…your theme song. You heard me. A theme song. During the late 1990s, a television show called *Ally McBeal* was all the rage. While I didn't really like it, there was one point I agreed with: everyone needs a theme song to make you feel better when the world gets you down. Now, it may be that in real life (as opposed to TV life), what you actually need is an entire playlist; moods and circumstances do change. But that's in the details.

Look: you've read this book. Great start. If you want it to really work for you, though—if you want to feel comfortable in your Aspie skin AND that you can speak some version of "Social-ease," you're going to need to read it again. And again. And you're going to need something to keep you moving when you feel you can't. Your theme song.

While you think about what your theme song should be, let me offer you mine. It's been my favorite song since I was about ten years old; it lifts me up, and it is, I hope, the legacy I leave with you: "Lean On Me" (the Club Nouveau version—download it and think of me). When the world has left you feeling tired or scared, unwanted or empty—you *can* lean on me. Lean on my pick-yourself-up-and-brush-yourself-off moments. Lean on the words in this book you're holding. I *will* be your friend when you feel alone—every time you grab this book, I will be there to help you move forward. Go out in the world. Try. Mess up. Try again. Be the quirky, unique, fabulous Aspie you're meant to be. Make this world better, funnier, kinder. Be silly, be intense. Be scared. Be brave. Be defiant. Be curious. And always, always, always—for all of us, Aspies—be glad, be proud. Be you.

Resources You Will Actually WANT to Use. Really

Because the more you know—the more you know.

For You...

We've talked about the hidden power of the words "manners, "lady," and "gentleman." By now, you know I'm not going to send you to Grandma's Miss Manners all of a sudden. These sources will give you the really particular details that we didn't cover, like arguing over the TV remote, managing "toiletiquette," flirting, and telling a friend his fly is open. They'll also help you explore things like friendship levels and flexible thinking in even more depth.

In Print

American Girl Library social books: Middleton, WI: American Girl

- Criswell, P.K. (2006) *Friends: Making Them and Keeping Them.*
- Criswell, P.K. (2008) *A Smart Girl's Guide to Friendship Troubles.*
- Criswell, P.K. (2008) *Stand Up for Yourself and Your Friends.*
- Criswell, P.K. (2011) *A Smart Girl's Guide to Knowing What to Say.*
- Madison, L. (2010) *The Care and Keeping of You Collection.*
- Phillips, B.W. (2009) *Oh Brother!...Oh Sister!: A Sister's Guide to Getting Along.*
- Timmons, B. (2005) *Yikes! A Smart Girl's Guide to Surviving Tricky, Sticky, Icky Situations.*
- Zelinger, L. (2012) *A Smart Girl's Guide to Liking Herself—Even on the Bad Days.*

Bridges, J. (2006) *50 Things Every Young Gentleman Should Know.* Nashville, TN: Thomas Nelson.

Cleary, N. (2001) *The Art and Power of Being a Lady.* New York: Atlantic Monthly Press.

Packer, A.J. (1997) *How Rude!: The Teenagers' Guide to Good Manners, Proper Behavior, and Not Grossing People Out.* St. Louis, MO: Turtleback School and Library Binding.

Winner, M.G. and Crooke, P. (2011) *Social Fate, Social Fortune.* San Jose, CA: Think Social Publishing.

Winner, M.G. and Crooke, P. (2011) *Socially Curious and Curiously Social: A Social Thinking Guidebook for Bright Teens and Young Adults.* Great Barrington, MA: North River Press.

Wiseman, R. (2010) *Boys, Girls and Other Hazardous Materials.* New York: G.P. Putman's Sons.

Online: Tumblr Blogs, Sites, Podcasts and Twitter Feeds

Etiquette for a Gentleman and Etiquette for a Lady
www.etiquettforagentleman.tmblr.com and *www.etiquettforalady.tumblr.com*
These are two of the most followed Tumblr blogs out there, and for good reason. Entries are one bite-sized, thoroughly modern truth at a time (like "If you loan a girl your sweatshirt, don't expect to get it back"). Smart guys and girls will follow BOTH.

iTwixie
www.itwixie.com
iTwixie is designed to empower and inspire tween girls "to change the world." A favorite of "Queen Bees" author, Rosalind Wiseman, the site aims to "challenge girls to express their unique talents, creations, natural beauty and true interests."

The Good Web Guide
www.thegoodwebguide.co.uk
Whether or not you live in the UK, the annual "short list" of fantastic websites spotlighted by thegoodwebguide are worth checking out and knowing about. Articles, links and videos will keep you up to date on trends in science, art, fashion, music, food and culture (everything from Jedi kittens to history podcasts); read/watch, and you will feel ready to talk about most anything. There's also a special section just for teens.

Modern Manners Guy: Quick and Dirty Tips for a More Polite Life
www.quickanddirtytips.com
From handling coffee house squatters to Apple Store etiquette, this is my favorite "of-the-moment" resource for an honest, funny and helpful take on modern "how-to's." You can follow host Richie Frieman on Twitter and Facebook, read his blog or even listen to his frequent (quick) podcasts.

(Actually, ALL of the Experts on "Quick and Dirty Tips" are worth your time—but they may not all relate to your life in particular…your choice on which to read and which to skip.)

Emily Post Online: Teen Scene
www.emilypost.com/teen-scene
Emily Post *is* the maven of all things mannerly. Her online teen site handles specifics like how to actually ask someone on a date, plan a party or avoid cafeteria food fights.

Stop Bullying
www.stopbullying.gov
Tips, tools and webisodes to help you deal with the real world stuff. Links to Cartoon Network's anti-bullying comic contests, too.

Bullying UK
www.bullying.co.uk
A digital poster creator, phone/skye support and advice for dealing with bullying online and at school.

Style for All!
Clothes
www.abercrombie.com, *www.boden.co.uk* and *www.bodenusa.com* (for both the UK and US sites: select "johnnie b" teen line) and *www.jcrew.com*
These are some of my favorite major (international) fashion sites for when you want that "young, neat and trendy" look the NT world tends to hold as most respectable. This doesn't have to be your fashion aesthetic—just as long as you know it is what generally is considered classic and stylish.

Guy Stuff
For the Young Dude (FTYD)
www.fortheyoungdude.com
Written by a 22-year-old guy with a knack for wit, this blog-a-zine (my word) covers everything a "young dude" needs to know: grooming, entertainment, design/technology, style and culture trends. You can also follow FTYD on Twitter, Tumblr and Facebook.

Beauty and Make-Up
Bobbi Brown
www.bobbibrowncosmetics.com and *www.prettypowerful.bobbibrowncosmetics.com*
This is a make-up campaign celebrating being pretty without make-up—or with. Your choice. Global make-up authority Bobbi Brown offers how-to's,

classic color palettes, fresh skin-care and the "be who you are" philosophy. (There's even a section under "Learn/Books" which will link you to Brown's bestsellers, *Makeup Manual*, *Beauty Rules* and *Teenage Beauty*.)

Dolly Bow Bow: Fashion. Beauty. Life.
www.dollybowbow.blogspot.com and *www.dollybowbow.co.uk*
The young, talented British jewelry designer behind Dolly Bow Bow (both blog and shop) was named one of the Top 22 Beauty Experts Under 22, and it shows. Her girlie-girl site is a visual feast of photography, video how-tos and trend suggestions.

Gift-Giving
Giving a spot-on gift takes a lot of attention and thought—the more you know about a person, the better the gift you choose will reflect his or her personality. It's how you show appreciation, affection and value for the people in your life. And a lot of Aspies find it really, really tough. So here's some help! These are some of my favorite sites for standout, creative, FUN gift-giving.

Etsy
www.etsy.com

Perpetual Kid
www.perpetualkid.com

UncommonGoods
www.uncommongoods.com

For Your Teachers, Parents and Family
In Print
(My first book is really the "other half" of this book. *Asperkids* is meant to give NTs a lesson (or two) in learning to speak Aspie. The better they understand you as you learn to better understand them…well, everything's just better for everyone.)

Cook O'Toole, J. (2012) *Asperkids: An Insider's Guide to Loving, Understanding and Teaching Children with Asperger Syndrome.* London: Jessica Kingsley Publishers.

Wiseman, R. (2009) *Queen Bees and Wannabes: Helping Your Daughter Survive Cliques, Gossip, Boyfriends, and the New Realities of Girl World.* New York: Three Rivers Press.

Online
Asperkids Online
www.asperkids.com
The web link to everything I can possibly think of to share with the adults in your life.

Social Thinking® Online
www.socialthinking.com
A bit of everything created by Michelle Garcia Winner and the idea of "thinking about you thinking about me." This is a great place to find all sorts of books and blogs.

Asperkids—Getting All Social On You
www.facebook.com/asperkids, www.pinterest.com/asperkids and *www.twitter.com/ asperkidstweets*
Inspiring quotes, important tools—plus Vulcans singing "The Police" and a Lego Princess Leia making photocopies of her bum. It's all here, and it's how I hope you'll stay connected with me.

References

Books

Attwood, T. (2007) *The Complete Guide to Asperger Syndrome*. London: Jessica Kingsley Publishers.

Carnegie, D. (1936) *How to Win Friends and Influence People*. New York: Simon & Schuster.

Fulgham, R. (2004) *All I Really Need to Know I Learned in Kindergarten* (15th anniversary edition). New York: Random House Publishing Group.

Henricks, R.G. (1989) Translation of original text by Lao Tzu. *Lao-Tzu: Te-Tao Ching*. New York: Ballantine Books.

Kennedy, L. (1992) *Business Etiquette for the Nineties: Your Ticket to Career Success*. South Carolina, SC: Palmetto Pub.

Seuss T.G. (1954) *Horton Hears a Who!* New York: Random House.

Vilord, T.J. (ed.) (2002) *1001 Motivational Quotes for Success*. Cherry Hill, NJ: Garden State Publishing.

White, E.B. (1952) *Charlotte's Web*. New York, NY: HarperCollins Publishers, Inc.

Whitman, W. "Song of Myself," in *Leaves of Grass*. Nashville, TN: American Renaissance.

Wiseman, R. (2009) *Queen Bees and Wannabes: Helping Your Daughter Survive Cliques, Gossip, Boyfriends, and the New Realities of Girl World*. New York: Three Rivers Press.

Online

Tumblr Blogs

Etiquette for a Gentleman and Etiquette for a Lady
www.etiquetteforagentleman.tumblr.com and *www.etiquetteforalady.tumblr.com*

Information and Resources

Social Thinking® Online
www.socialthinking.com

Media

"The Friendship Algorithm" on *The Big Bang Theory*. Warner Brothers Television. Written by Chuck Lorre, 19 January 2009.

"Lean On Me" (1972) Written and originally recorded by Bill Withers. Club Nouveau version released in 1987.

Phineas and Ferb. Disney Channel Original Productions.

Personal Communication

Dr. Irm Bellavia ("Hold the Pillow" concept), Adolescent and Pediatric Psychiatry, Charlotte, NC, May, 2011.

Quotation Pages Sources

BrainyQuote

www.brainyquote.com

Database includes referenced quotes by Henry Ford, Ralph Waldo Emerson and Alan Alda.

SearchQuotes

www.searchquotes.com

Database includes referenced quote by Maya Angelou.